hat ways the heroic attempts of these
great synthesizers " (Hermann, Schweit-
er, Bultmann, and Tillich) failed, re-
ulting in the breakdown of Protestant
holarly piety and an experience of men-
al and spiritual separation that led
raight to the rise of the radicals.

n his examination of the work of Altizer,
Hamilton, van Buren, and Cox, Dr. Coo-
er discusses the meaning of the phrase,
God is dead," criticizes the positions of
ltizer and Hamilton, and clarifies Til-
ch's connection with the radical theol-
gy. " The essential element in the ' God
dead ' culture," he says, " is our com-
on sense of the loss of the conviction of
od's hope for human self-transcen-
ence." Viewing the radical attempts to
cover this sense of transcendence (in-
luding Teilhard de Chardin's), Dr.
ooper urges that theology should re-
ond positively and constructively to
e " death of God " movement, and con-
udes that our present theological situa-
on is such that " only the most radical
ttempts to recover the sense of the
cred . . . have any chance of success."

THE AUTHOR

OHN CHARLES COOPER is a gradu-
te of the University of South Carolina
B.A.), Lutheran Theological Southern
eminary (B.D.), Lutheran School of
heology, Chicago (St.M.), and the Uni-
ersity of Chicago (M.A. and Ph.D.). He
s Associate Professor of Philosophy and
Iead of the Philosophy Department,
Newberry College, South Carolina.

The Roots
of the Radical Theology

The Roots
of the Radical Theology

by

JOHN CHARLES COOPER

THE WESTMINSTER PRESS
Philadelphia

LIBRARY OF CONGRESS CATALOG CARD No. 67–12013

1 Theology, Doctrinal -- History -- 19th Century
2 Theology, Doctrinal -- History -- 20th Century
3 Death of God theology

Published by The Westminster Press®
Philadelphia, Pennsylvania

PRINTED IN THE UNITED STATES OF AMERICA

This book is dedicated to my wife, Ann,
in gratitude for all the inspiration and help
she gave me in its writing

Contents

Preface

This book grew out of the exciting discussions that took place at Emory University in the fall of 1965 during the conference on America and the Future of Theology, and out of the meetings of the Southern Section of the American Academy of Religion at Columbia Theological Seminary, Decatur, Georgia, in March, 1966. At both of these conferences the radical theology that proclaims the "death of God" was presented and defended against many attacks by Thomas J. J. Altizer. This writer took an active part in the exploration of the meaning of the new theology at both conferences, and presented an appreciative yet critical paper addressed to Thomas Altizer at the later meeting. It was an intention then, and it is the intention of this book, to *understand* the genetic development of this new trend in Christian thought in a positive way. It is not my intention to attack or to defend radical theology. Rather, the aim of this study is to lay bare some of the reasons why the radical theology has arisen in our time. Once these reasons are discussed, the final judgment of this work should be clear. That judgment is that the radical theology *is* a fruitful way for religious thought to move in our common search for a recovery of the sense of personal self-transcendence and the dimension of the transcendent in our day.

Without personally affirming the death of God — indeed, even in rejecting the most recent interpretation put upon the

concept by Altizer and Hamilton — I maintain that the radical
theology is the most promising theological movement now at
work. Only radical thought that cuts to the roots of our current
religious problems can point us toward a recovery of the transcendent dimensions of life. Only radical answers are suitable
to radical questions, and even when the answers of the new
theology are wrong, they (unlike the answers of more orthodox theologians) are not irrelevant. It is hoped that these pages
will make clear the relevance of the new theology to the problems of modern life as well as demonstrate its inevitability.

Meanwhile, in the presence of God's silence we wait in hope
and love for the once-living experience of transcendence to
become available again, believing that the God of the future
will be all that the God of the past once was, but is not now
for our culture. In that hope we live, recognizing the signs of
God's past activity (or the signs of the promise of the recovery
of the transcendent) in the Christlike love of thousands of
sensitive men and women everywhere. Our faith remains un-
shaken in the declaration of John that if the Nameless One can
be named, that Name is Love.

J. C. C.

Newberry College
Newberry, South Carolina

Introduction

This is a book about Western radical religious thought. It is a survey of the contrapuntal or negatively critical developments in Western philosophy and theology that have influenced the development of our own way of looking at the world, which we call our historical self-consciousness. This is not a book for the defensive-minded, for the author is decisively committed to the critical tradition and makes no attempt to defend the "orthodox" position in regard to faith or reason. Yet it is a positive book, a great yea-saying that has built itself up upon a large number of nay-sayings to the more comfortable way of affirming the *status quo* in church and state. This book makes no claim of infallibility; it is simply one way — an open-minded way — of assessing the movement of Christian thought. It is not a complete book either, for while it begins with ancient philosophy, it moves quickly to the era of the Enlightenment and devotes most of its attention to the late eighteenth century and after in its establishment of the modern theological tradition. It is a book that unashamedly has "heroes" too. Schleiermacher, Kant, Kierkegaard, Herrmann, Schweitzer, Bultmann, Tillich, Bonhoeffer, Teilhard de Chardin, and men like them who cared for Christianity and labored to make it a genuine force in human life are presented respectfully to the present age for serious consideration. The most radical radicals are respectfully handled too. Altizer, Hamilton, van Buren,

Cox, and others are taken for what they are — young and concerned theologians who have something to say to our generation. But, with all the respect paid to heroes and all the seriousness given to young radicals, they come in for criticism, too.

In brief, this book is developed in a chronological way. Chapter I deals with the definition of, and the development of, the critical tradition in Western culture. It deals with the Greeks, with Jesus, with Luther, and with the radical philosophers of the eighteenth and nineteenth centuries. Beginning with Chapter II, the balance of the book is concerned with the late eighteenth, nineteenth, and twentieth centuries. First, the contribution of critical scholarship to the breakdown or rationalistic orthodoxy is traced (Chapter II), then the efforts of liberal scholars to provide a piety available to modern men is discussed (Chapter III). The heroic efforts of these liberal "synthesizers" — Herrmann, Schweitzer, Bultmann, and Tillich — are shown to be failures, and Chapter IV passes on to a description of the breakdown of Protestant scholarly piety. This breakdown leads straight to the rise of the radicals, who are treated in Chapter V. In conclusion, the elements that provoked the rise of radical theology (the "death of God" movement) and some indications of the possible future of theology are given in Chapter VI.

In the course of this book, we shall investigate most of the developments in modern theology. The so-called quest for the historical Jesus, the struggle between liberalism and fundamentalism, the demythologizing movement, religionless Christianity, the civil rights struggle, and the "death of God" theology will all be discussed in connection with the historical influences that brought them into being. We shall not attempt to explain the rise of modern radical thought by speaking of our age as one of apostasy, or by tracing the cry "God is dead" back to Nietzsche and dropping the matter there. Rather, we shall identify the breaking point of the orthodox religious tradition in the West as the Enlightenment of the eighteenth century, and develop the basis of modern radical thought out of a study of the philosophy and theology that followed Immanuel Kant and Friedrich Schleiermacher.

Our survey of the sources of modern radical thought will close with a discussion of the background of our day's chief theological problem, the question of God, which we shall identify as an almost universal sense of the loss of the element of self-transcendence in human life. We shall see that this problem is of such a serious nature that only the most radical attempts to recover a sense of the sacred and the experience of self-transcendence have any chance of success. It is our hope that this book, by honestly setting forth the historical origins of our present situation, may serve as a stimulus to religious men today, that they may join in the quest for the recovery of that sense of the sacred and the transcending which might still be found in the midst of the flux and problems of human life. If this quest is made, we may yet discover a historical resurrection of the experience of the sacred even though we have lived through the death of the Divine conceived under mythological symbols.

Chapter I
The Contrapuntal Tradition in the West

THE TWENTIETH CENTURY in the West is marked by one great achievement of the nineteenth century — historical self-consciousness. So marked by this outlook is our century that it probably is a truism that the popular world view of any era runs at least one hundred years behind the insights of the professional thinker. Our era, by which we mean the educated people of Europe and America in our time, understands itself in terms of its historical development in a way that only small groups of individuals ever achieved in past centuries. Hegel, Marx, and Darwin may be only names to countless thousands of people living today, but the advent of universal education, the printing of millions of books, and the discovery and exploitation of great networks of mass communication have made their ideas — and the ideas of other nineteenth-century thinkers — the property of the millions. The question most often asked by people today is not the ontological question of the early philosophers, Where did we come from? but the genetic, developmental question of the historian and the sociologist, How did we get this way? Ours is an era that looks for the underlying processes of change, not for unchanging principles and structures. Alfred North Whitehead, with his emphasis upon the relationship of the past to the present and the future, is typical of our century. The thirst of Plato to uncover the unchanging world of reality — beyond the flux of historical change

— is well-nigh unintelligible to most of us. Every schoolboy, and certainly every college student, is at least exposed to this kind of thinking. Most college programs attempt to impart a sensitivity to the historical processes that have produced the world situation in which we dwell today. The student quickly orients himself to his place in the panorama of conscious and unconscious forces that are sweeping on from the past, through the instantaneous moment of decision that is the present, into the openness of the future. And this orientation is full-orbed, having literary, religious, biological, and scientific elements as well as historical and political aspects. Unconsciously, if not consciously, we soon begin to understand ourselves as the latest event in a series of related events that lead backward from the second just past to the dimmest reaches of the pre-history of an expanding universe. All is in process, all is in motion, and time itself is moving forward bearing the ripples that we have caused in it toward the ultimate condition, maximum entropy, when all processes will stop because of the maximum distribution of atomic energy. But that event is far away, and meanwhile we can affect the flux of life and can participate in the ceaseless change that engulfs us and that produced us. Our actions can — and do — have consequences because we are the stuff of which the future is being made. Perhaps, because of our insights, because of our protests and reforms, because of our deeds, the future of man can be richer, more peaceful, more conducive to the development of the human spirit. Such is the understanding and the resolution of the best of our young people, and it is a good understanding within its own limitations.

When we cast our glance over the history of Western culture from the sixth century before Christ until now, a startling insight emerges. That insight is that the critic of one era often becomes the foundation stone of the next. The observation of many young people in our day and for many decades past is that the heresy of one period amusingly becomes the orthodoxy of another. The distinctively constructive element in Western culture has, more often than not, proved to be the great critics and nay-sayers of prior generations. Borrowing from Hegel, we might observe that it has been the antitheses to the thesis of an age that has provoked the birth of a finer synthesis in later times. The criticism and negative assessments of any period of thought have often proved to be the genuine source of positive human progress.

Almost anyone can cite the historical examples upon which the above insight is based. Thales was thought mad when he predicted that an eclipse of the sun would occur in May, 585 B.C. When his prediction turned out to be correct, he was hailed as a god, but he refused the divine honors and began to found Western philosophy. Heraclitus (ca. 500 B.C.), one of the keenest philosophical minds of all time, despised the people of his city, saying that their attitude was, "We will have none that is best among us; if there be any such, let him be so elsewhere and among others."

Xenophanes (sixth century B.C.) savagely attacked the philosophy and theology of his day, criticizing the pantheon of Homer as the making of gods in the image of man. "Homer and Hesiod," he tells us, "have ascribed to the gods all things that are a shame and a disgrace among mortals, stealings, adulteries, and deceivings of one another." Xenophanes flayed the Greek anthropomorphism, saying that if the oxen or lions had gods, they would form them as oxen or lions. In place of all that crudity, Xenophanes proclaimed that there is "one god, the greatest among gods and men, neither in form like unto mortals nor in thought. He sees all over, thinks all over, and hears all over." Xenophanes thus offered, in his criticism, a view of God that approaches the loftiness of the Hebrew prophets. The heresy of one age proved to be the orthodoxy of another.

Every student of Western civilization would place heavy emphasis upon the ugly, popeyed figure of Socrates, the little sculptor who heard voices. Socrates stood steadfast against the shallowness of the culture of Athens in his day — the years 470 B.C. to 399 B.C., which are considered high points in our cultural development. Socrates conceived of his philosophical task as twofold. On the one hand he was a "midwife," helping men to give birth to their own ideas, but on the other he was a "gadfly," stinging the great sleepy beast that was the Athenian state. It was because of his "gadfly" activities that the state eventually brought Socrates to trial and sentenced him to drink the hemlock reserved for the most terrible enemies of the people. It is a commonplace that the treasons and heresies of Socrates became the principal glory of the Greek people — and that only a generation or two later.

Socrates' god was the god who is discovered by human reason, not one of the gods of popular Greek thought, although Socrates referred to him as Apollo. Tried for the mixed charge of being an atheist and of being "a setter forth of foreign divinities" (one of history's greatest contradictions), Socrates was found guilty on both counts. Yet, at his trial, Socrates said: "I do believe [in god] in a sense in which none of my accusers does" (*Apology*, 34B–36B). Socrates remained to the end the pious heretic who maintained, "I will obey the god rather than you, gentlemen"; "I will never cease being a philosopher" (*Apology*, 27D–29E). Four hundred and fifty years later, when Paul came to Athens, he was to find the people of that day admirers of Socrates who still put his spirit to death. For when Paul proclaimed the Christ, the Athenians assessed Paul as a "setter forth of foreign divinities" and ignored him (Acts 17:18). Sometimes the person of the heretic is venerated by a later age, while the freedom of his spirit is still suspect. It may be easier to gain popularity than influence upon the generations of men. Yet the world has never forgotten Socrates and his method of cross-examination. Nor have all men forgotten his assertion that the philosopher best benefits mankind when he discomforts it.

After Socrates, Greek culture produced men who were conscious gadflies, patterning their lives upon Socrates. The Cynics, with their antisocial behavior, rejected the ethics and the hypocrisy of Greek society. They were the " beats " of the centuries before Christ, living by the prayer of Socrates, who asked: " O great Pan, . . . grant me beauty in the inner man and only so much gold as the wise can carry." The cynic revolt against life as it was lived then culminated in the unwashed figure of the reformed counterfeiter, Diogenes, who slept in a tub. When Alexander the Great stood over the sunbathing Diogenes and respectfully asked if there was anything he could do for him, Diogenes asked only that Alexander step out of his sunlight. Later centuries that venerated the austerities of the Christian monks, who fled to the desert to battle the world, the flesh, and the devil, actually venerated that which was Diogenes-like in them.

In the movement of history, the reign of Caesar Augustus arrived, and in Palestine a lowly Jew was born. The figure of that Jew, who lived only thirty-three years, has dominated the thought world and the cultural forms of the West ever since. The Jesus of history was a striking religious reformer, a radical thinker who not only challenged but replaced the central foundations of his inherited faith. Whatever other value we may individually put upon this man — and millions, living and dead, have called him the manifestation of God in history — we must acknowledge him as the seminal figure of Western culture. Yet, in the words of the Fourth Evangelist, " He came unto his own and his own received him not." The net effect of Jesus' preaching was the conversion of a small group that accepted his beliefs about God, and the rejection of his message by the leaders and the great masses of his people. The cross may remind us of a positive sign at this historical remove, but in its own time it stood like a negative sign of judgment upon the Hebrew religion. The fact that Jesus was accepted as the Christ, the self-manifestation of God, by millions of Europeans later does not erase the basic fact that he was a heretic in his own time. The combined weight of the examples of Socrates and of Jesus makes it an obvious insight that the great critics have been the truly constructive personalities in the progress of Western culture. Centuries before Jesus, the prophet Jeremiah expressed the key to the historical development of religion:

> See [says the Lord], I have set you this day
>   over nations and over kingdoms,
> to pluck up and to break down,
> to destroy and to overthrow,
> to build and to plant.

(Jer. 1:10.)

The Contrapuntal Tradition in Later Times

We do not need to belabor our point concerning the value of negativity toward the culture (and religion) of one's day by citing examples from the whole range of Western history. If we move over the centuries from Christ to the Reformation period, we may find other examples of "positive negativity" that may give us a deeper insight into the value of the cultural and theological critics of our own day. The date A.D. 1517 brings us to that melancholy divine, the German peasant-theologian, Martin Luther.

There may be churchmen who would take exception to our reference to Jesus as a critic, or a "radical," which only shows how completely Jesus' radicality has become accepted as normative, but few people would differ when we identify Luther as a radical critic of his church and culture. Theologians and historians have given Luther the title "the conservative Reformer," but such a tag can make sense only in relation to some other Reformers who kicked over more of the medieval heritage than Luther did. Relative to Thomas Müntzer, who wanted to create a paradise on earth by abolishing private property and the institution of marriage, Luther was a "conservative radical," but in relation to the Catholic Church and most of

Christendom, Luther was a really radical radical. It may help many of us today to take a look at Luther from the standpoint of the bulk of Christendom in the sixteenth century and see the threat incorporated in his critique as Luther's own age saw it. One thing is sure, Luther did not effect the breakup of Western Christendom and begin the Protestant tradition by preaching in favor of the *status quo* or by counseling the sixteenth-century equivalent of "gradual integration."

The facts are that Luther lived in an age of radical reassessment. Luther's age had to be, for Islam, in the form of Turkish imperialism, was on the march and had struck deep into the heart of Europe. Islam was at the outskirts of Vienna throughout most of the events of Luther's life. Luther really was a radical, for he undertook programs that effectively split Christendom in one of its darkest hours. Perhaps a fanciful parallel might be seen if we imagine someone stirring up a war between North and South in the United States while the Chinese were invading San Francisco. Luther may not — and probably did not — intend to create such a condition, but his actions had that effect. Only the political common sense of the Holy Roman Emperor and the German princes caused the two factions to reunite in the face of the Turkish threat. It is all very well to put up statues to outstanding men, but let us not forget that most of them were radical critics in their own times.

The theological thrust of Luther's Reformation is best summed up in his own agonizing question: "How can I get me a merciful God?" Luther was a deeply pious man; he was more a man of the Middle Ages than of the "modern" period which he, in some sense, began. Well educated, with good prospects in life as a lawyer, a religious experience — of the fear of the God who hated sin — sent him to the monastery. Once there, Luther sought peace of soul through religious "works," fasting, praying, working. But peace did not come to Luther through the means of grace built into the medieval church, and he sank into deep melancholy. That depression was cut short and reversed — becoming a sense of liberation and joy — by Luther's "tower experience," in which his mind broke through to a fresh understanding of the grace and love of God. Contrary to popular expositions of this experience, Luther found his peace in Matt. 4:17 rather than in Rom. 1:17. As Luther writes in the Ninety-five Theses of 1517, the light broke when he became sure about the meaning of the word "repent" in the New Testament. Luther had been taught that this word meant that one was to "do penitence," to do religious works such as fasting and praying. In his new knowledge — gained from studies in the Greek text of the New Testament — Luther saw that "repent" meant "to change one's mind," to "turn oneself around" and begin to live differently than one had in the past. This lifelong process of repentance was possible to accept, whereas in "doing penitence," one was never sure how much penitence — if any — was enough for salvation. Luther's radical break with the sacramental-penitential system of the medieval church was thus a recovery of the "freedom we have in Christ" taught by Paul. The man who would be justified was to live in faith, constantly striving to turn toward Christ and away from selfishness and disobedience to God.

In the Ninety-five Theses, Luther said:

When our Lord and Master Jesus Christ said "Repent" (Matthew 4:17) he wills that the entire life of believers to be one of repentance. (First thesis.)

After he had gained this insight, Luther could make sense of "The just shall live by faith" in Rom. 1:17.

It would be anticlimactic to point out that Luther's criticism of the church of his day became the orthodoxy of a great part of Europe within a few generations of his death. The recent movements toward "reformation" expressed by the Roman Catholic Second Vatican Council reveal the renewal of interest in Luther by the very descendants of those who read him out of the Catholic Church. The radical of 1517 has become the foundation stone of the renewal of orthodoxy in later centuries. The example of Luther ought to make our age more tolerant of the radical in our own time, since historical self-consciousness and appreciation of past events are part of our way of looking at the world. The heritage of Luther's radicality is not missing from the "God is dead" controversy of our own times, for the philosopher Nietzsche credits the phrase "God is dead" to one of Luther's hymns! Of course, in Luther, the phrase was a dramatic statement about the sacrifice of Christ on the cross, but Luther really believed that when Christ died, God died in some sense. So much a part of Luther was this phrase that once when he was sunk in deep gloom his wife Catherine chided him: "You look as if God were dead." Later in our treatment of radical thought we shall return to Luther's influence again. In the remainder of this chapter we shall discuss the modern Secular Critics of the Mainstream of Western Thought.

Auguste Comte and Positivism

Auguste Comte (1798–1857) was one of those critical personalities whose efforts to institutionalize his insights into life failed, but who decisively affected the development of Western thought by the sheer radicality of his message. A socialist and a humanist, Comte never lost the religious drive for some sort of salvation. He even sought to form a kind of "church," based on his view of science, which venerated humanity in place of a transcendental God, and substituted the glorious company of the philosophers and scientists for the glorious company of the apostles and the holy catholic church. "The Religion of Humanity," as an institution, died with Comte, but his ideas and ideals have never died. Comte's change of man's angle of vision from eternity to time, from the divine to the human, is a basic element in that historical self-consciousness which we have identified as the modern world view.

Comte was a radical's radical, for he concluded from his

studies that reform or reassessment of the elements in Western culture was not enough. The chief problem of his age (as he saw it) was the problem of the conflict between science and religion. There were three ways in which this problem might be solved. First, an attempt to reconcile science and religion might be made. Secondly, the church might be declared above the criticisms of science, and scholarship might be placed under the discipline of the church. Finally, science might be transformed, through a philosophical exposition of its leading ideas, into a substitute religion. Comte chose the third way out. He proposed a religion of humanity based on a science of social behavior. Sociology was born, then, as a new gospel designed to replace the old.

Comte's view of history was essentially evolutionary in that he believed that the "modern" situation, in which science was to replace religious modes of thought, had evolved out of earlier stages when such religious thought was possible and necessary. Mankind's world view changes, taught Comte, moving through a process of growth from theological forms, when the world is explained as the arena of God's activity; to philosophical or metaphysical forms, when the world is explained in terms of the movement of being and nonbeing; to the scientific form, which recognizes laws in nature and society. The "modern," scientific form of world view, Comte called positivism. Positivism, which still undergirds much of our philosophical thinking today, essentially holds that there are no beings or structures (gods or heavens or hells) that exist apart from the universe we experience through the senses. There is only one world, the world of phenomena in motion, of causes and effects, which is open to scientific investigation. The world view of our own day still retains the imprint of Comte's positivism in those elements of our common philosophy which see the world as all on one level — the material level — and understand the universe in monochromatic, unidimensional terms. As Rudolf Bultmann has expressed this philosophical presupposition, we are no longer able to believe seriously in a three-decker universe. No seriously concerned person believes in a heaven up there and a hell down there anymore.

Comte and his pathetic attempt to ape the Catholic Church by the creation of a religion of humanity failed, but the radical singularity of his vision has become our way — with all the limitations it implies — of looking at the world.

Ludwig Feuerbach and the Essence of Christianity

Ludwig Feuerbach (1804–1872) stands just behind the scenes of history, one of those important influences on human thought who remain unknown to the masses of men because their influence is exercised through the medium of other men. Feuerbach, a nineteenth-century philosopher with a deep interest in Christian theology, made a sweeping philosophical transformation of theology into anthropology. In other words, Feuerbach declared that in every religious assertion we make, we are talking about man and his qualities and not about God. " God," for Feuerbach, is the great depository of human possibilities and values.

Feuerbach did not think of himself as an atheist; on the contrary, by his own definition he was not. Feuerbach simply gave a completely naturalistic (and humanistic) interpretation of " theology." While Feuerbach produced no school of disciples, he, like Comte, decisively influenced the future. No less a believer in the " reality " of the supernatural than Karl Barth has testified to the greatness and the thoroughness of Feuerbach's vision. According to Barth, there are only two alternatives in our faith life: the way of Feuerbach or the way of belief in the Biblical self-manifestation of God. Of course, Barth sees Feuerbach as the clearest example of the wrong way to approach Christian faith, and thus values his system chiefly as a warning to twentieth-century men. Barth has founded his own theology (written in many large volumes of the *Church Dogmatics*) on the reality of revelation, and completely rejects " religion " as a human effort to reach God. Barth, along with Feuerbach, thus feels that to believe in religion is to believe in man, and in man's potentialities to save himself. Barth therefore declares such a belief in religion to be wrong, while Feuerbach considered it to be the only way open to man.

What Feuerbach did was to shift the theological referent from the objective to the subjective. Doctrines, for Feuerbach, are subjective in their origin, the crystallization of mankind's inward hopes, fears, and desires. Those qualities and aspects of life which mankind has come to value most — love, cooperation, sacrifice of self for others — are idealized, and, cast into pictures, are called (taken together) God and his attributes. Behind these idealizations there is no objective reality. God does not " exist," except as the projection of man's inner hopes and values. Man thus creates God, instead of God creating man.

It is not surprising that the man who gave such a radical reassessment of religion was never allowed to hold a chair of philosophy in a nineteenth-century university. Feuerbach served as a " private tutor " at Erlangen University for a while, but later retired to his own home to write his books. Feuerbach once announced that his purpose was to change " the friends of God into friends of man, believers into thinkers, worshippers into workers, candidates for the other world into students of this world, Christians who on their own confession are half-animal and half-angel, into men — whole men." [1]

Two things become clear when we examine Feuerbach's ambitious program and its fortunes throughout the century since he proposed it. The first fact that emerges is that the church, with its transcendental message, is still here. Feuerbach did not convince most Christian believers and theologians of the rightness of his program. In fact, the end of the nineteenth century and the early decades of the twentieth century witnessed the rise of a crude Biblical literalism in fundamentalism, and, after 1918, the rise of a sophisticated neo-orthodoxy under the influence of Karl Barth, Emil Brunner, and the Niebuhr brothers. Barth and Brunner, and their allies in Germany and America, have largely dominated the theological scene from 1920 to 1950, just because they emphasized the transcendental elements of grace and God's reality apart from the world and man that Feuerbach most wanted to humanize.

But the rejection of Feuerbach's views by the leading theologians of our century is not the whole story. Actually, beliefs about religion that are similar to Feuerbach's are widespread. The psychological theories of religion, put forward by Sigmund Freud and others, bear great resemblance to the theories of Feuerbach. Almost every religious thinker in our century recognizes that the kind of projection of human values which Feuerbach discussed does operate at least on some levels of the religious life. Aside from any decision about the reality of God apart from the world, theologians recognize that believers often project onto the image of God the hopes and desires of their nation and social class. The God of the white supremacists of Mississippi and South Africa, who "demand" racial segregation, is a case in point. Thus Feuerbach's overall program may have been rejected, but some of his insights have become part of the intellectual equipment of the Christian thinker.

Feuerbach's efforts were more successful than the rejection he received in life would indicate. It was Feuerbach who pioneered the use of the terms "I and Thou" in the description of the religious relationship. Martin Buber, the famous Jewish philosopher and theologian, has immortalized this manner of speaking, which most Christian theologians have hastened to adopt. Feuerbach declared, "The true dialectic is no monologue of the lonely thinker with himself, it is a dialogue between I and Thou." [2]

But Feuerbach's greatest influence on the world outlook of the twentieth century has been through the drastic transformation of the thinking of millions of men brought about through the spread of Marxism. Karl Marx read Feuerbach's works and formed his own atheistic evaluation of religion on Feuerbach's model. For Marx, religion was indeed a projection of man's subjective desires, but with a vast difference in value from the positive value placed on religion by Feuerbach. Feuerbach believed religion to be good, to be an expression of the noblest desires of men. Marx believed religion to be just the opposite. For Marx, religion is the projection of the values and the self-interest of the ruling classes, who then use the threats and promises of religion to keep the working classes in subjection to them. Thus, for Marx, religion is another instrument for repressing the poor, and must be overthrown, just as monarchies and police forces must be overthrown. It is only fair to Feuerbach to state that he had no such ideas about religion, but such has been the use of his insights by Marx and Marxists.

Looked at in terms of the influence of Marxist ideas and activities upon the religious institutions of Europe, Feuerbach must be accorded the title of a major influence upon the twentieth century. Nineteenth-century Germany tried to ignore and isolate the insights of Feuerbach, but that is the one thing man cannot do to an idea. It is possible to twist and distort the ideals and ideas of history's great radicals — as Marx has done — or to adopt only those parts of a man's insights which are agreeable to your own outlook — as Buber and other theologians have done — but it is not possible to act as if those insights were never given voice. "The stone which the builders rejected has become the head of the corner" is a judgment that the processes of history have passed on unpopular ideas again and again.

Friedrich Nietzsche and the Great Reversal

The dialectical tension in which Nietzsche (1844–1900) has been held, both in his own time and throughout the philosophical and theological developments of the twentieth century, needs little documentation. By " dialectical tension," we mean the paradoxical position in which Nietzsche has placed all thinkers after him of having to say " yes " and " no " to his insights at the same time. Nietzsche's dialectic lay deep within himself, and his own life may be the best commentary on his teachings. Nietzsche was an ill man. Throughout his life there runs a thread of illness, severe headaches, and psychosomatic problems of various kinds. At the age of fifty-four, he suffered a terminal mental breakdown. His life ended in a madhouse. Such is the paradoxical background of the man who brought to clearest expression the concept of the strong man armed who would conquer the world — not only physically but spiritually as well. Out of his rejection of sickness and weakness, Nietzsche fashioned the ideal of the superman.

For Nietzsche, the superman was something eschatological, that is, something that was coming soon that would shatter the structures of society and philosophy as men knew them in the late nineteenth century. The superman would be the man who would openly claim to be God — a " knowledge " that had been available to mankind for centuries, and that had found expression in Comte and Feuerbach. Like Marx, Nietzsche identified God as a projection of society's ideals and self-interests. God was an ideal and an idol that hung over men as an invisible threat. The Father stands for all those repressions upon the vital powers of man which decline if they are repressed.

Nietzsche thus proclaimed what was to him a gospel, a good news of release and liberation: " Before God! Now however this God has died! Ye higher men, this God was your greatest danger. Only since he lay in the grave have ye again arisen. Now only cometh the great noontide, now only doth the higher man become — master! . . . Well! Take heart! Ye higher men! Now only travaileth the mountain of the human future. God hath died: Now do we desire — the Superman to live." [3]

Nietzsche thus proclaimed the death of one God, but the coming birth of another. Perhaps he let out his secret longing for the substitution of a god that idealized and promoted human values and desires — for example, the drive for power and self-expression — when he wrote later in the same chapter as the above quotation: "For the great despisers are the great reverers." [4]

Nietzsche left no disciples, but he has left his impress upon all twentieth-century thought. The "master race" idea of Nazism, which was one philosophic concept that was put into the most extreme concrete form by the insanity of Hitler and his cohorts, cannot be blamed entirely on Nietzsche's thought, but it was based on it in part. The identification of the superman with the northern European racial stock was not made by Nietzsche, but it was a simple identification to make.

Yet Nietzsche's most pervasive influence on twentieth-century thought has just surfaced in the theological thinking of the last decade. This influence is the valuation placed on Nietzsche as a prophet of the religious sensibility by the radical theologians of "the death of God" movement. As Nietzsche wrote: "Even God hath his hell: it is his love for man. . . . God is dead: of his pity for man hath God died." [5]

Now, the startling announcement that God is dead, proclaimed by Christian thinkers such as Thomas J. J. Altizer and William Hamilton, can have several meanings. Even the harshness of the phrase (and its apparent illogicality) can be so interpreted that the majority of Christians can get some "value" from it. Thus it is of interest to discover just which interpretation Altizer and Hamilton put on the phrase. The phrase, we all know, is from Nietzsche, but that means little by way of influence. However, *if the interpretation put on the phrase is also from Nietzsche,*[6] we have a demonstrable influence of the "great despiser" and radical thinker on the theological thought of our own time.

First, let us describe the range of possible meanings that the phrase "God is dead" may have; then let us look for any possible influence of Nietzsche.

In *Radical Theology and the Death of God,* coauthored by Altizer and Hamilton,[7] we are told:

Nor should the phrase " death of God " be linked to Nietzsche alone, for in one way or another it lies at the foundation of a distinctly modern thought and experience. [8]

The authors then move on to a description of various ways in which the phrase may be understood, ways that range from " conventional atheism to theological orthodoxy." [9]

The first meaning is that there is no God and that there never has been. This is traditional atheism, and it is rejected by the authors.

The second meaning is that there once was a God to whom worship was appropriate, but now there is no such God. This meaning is explicitly identified as the position of Altizer and Hamilton. We shall return to this interpretation and discuss it fully below.

The third meaning is that the idea of God and the word " God " itself are in need of radical reformulation. New words may be needed to refer to God (Paul Tillich's position), or a decent silence about God may be necessary (the position of Harvey Cox in *The Secular City* [10] and of Tillich in *The Courage to Be* [11]).

The fourth meaning is that our traditional religious language needs to be revised, but the fundamental reality, God, remains real. This is the " soft " interpretation of radical ideas, which expresses itself in various efforts to " revise " the liturgy of the church, to minister to teen-agers in their own argot, etc.

The fifth possible meaning of the phrase " God is dead " may be that the Christian story no longer has the power to save or to heal men. This view holds that the symbols of Christ and his cross, of the Nativity and the resurrection, have lost their power to move us toward social and personal integrity. As Paul Tillich has observed in *The Dynamics of Faith,*[12] religious symbols are born, live, and die among social groups. When the situation of the symbol-creating group (Western mankind) changes, then the symbol may die. That is what this possible meaning of the phrase denotes to some people.

A sixth alternative meaning of the phrase of Nietzsche may be the interpretation first put forward by William Hamilton in *The New Essence of Christianity*.[13] In that radical work, Hamilton proposed that the modern world view no longer allows us to believe honestly that God is the problem solver for us. Hamilton says that we have to face the fact that we look to science for the help that past generations asked from God. Thus certain concepts of God must go, like those held by the Breton fishermen who prayed, "O God, thy ocean is so great and my boat is so small." Other ways of talking about God must be fashioned, according to this view, or we must stop "God talk" altogether.

The seventh alternative meaning of the phrase "God is dead" is the argument about the silence of God spoken of by Dietrich Bonhoeffer in his *Letters and Papers from Prison*.[14] Bonhoeffer suggested that "religious people speak of God when human perception is [often just from laziness] at an end, or human resources fail."[15] He went on to suggest that such "lazy" talk is just a "seeking frantically to make room for God."[16] In place of this kind of loose talk, Bonhoeffer suggested that "the Pauline question" today is "the question whether religion is a condition of salvation."[17] He was quick to go on to say: "Freedom from circumcision is at the same time freedom from religion. I ask myself why a Christian instinct frequently draws me more to the religionless than to the religious."[18] Bonhoeffer's justly famous argument, then, is to the effect that God is now silent, and we men should be silent about him.

"God is teaching us that we must live as men who can get along very well without him. The God who is with us is the God who forsakes us. . . . The God who makes us live in this world without using him as a working hypothesis is the God before whom we are ever standing." [19]

The eighth possible meaning of Nietzsche's phrase is that men make their own gods or idols in every age, and these false gods must die and be forgotten so that the True Divinity might emerge, might be reborn in our religious life. This extremely "soft" interpretation sounds like the message of Luther ("Every man has either the true God or an Idol"), or like some of the propaganda against polytheism in the Old Testament ("The gods of the heathens are idols of wood and stone"). That there is an element of truth in this view, with respect to every generation, we do not deny. But this is too weak an interpretation to draw from the assertion that "God is dead."

The ninth possible interpretation of the word about "the death of God" is a mystical one. This quite old insight is the view that God must die in the world so that he can be born in us, a death associated with Jesus' death on the cross.

Finally, Altizer and Hamilton suggest a tenth interpretation of the phrase "God is dead" which holds that it means no more than that our language about the Divine is always inadequate and imperfect. This hardly seems like a possible interpretation, since every theologian and philosopher is aware of the analogical and equivocal nature of the language men use about God. [20]

Altizer and Hamilton declare that the second possible meaning — that there once was a God who rightly was worshiped but now there is no such God — is their position. [21] We must confess that such an interpretation is difficult to understand! This is truly "an atheist position with a difference." [22] Yet there is one way in which we can understand Altizer's and Hamilton's latest version of the meaning of the phrase "God is dead," and that is by reference to Nietzsche's *Thus Spake Zarathustra*, where we read: "God is dead; of his pity for man hath God died." [23]

This does not explain what it means to say that there once was a God but there is no longer. It does, however, reveal the source of the insights of these radical thinkers, and it gives us a clue to an interpretation of the radical theology that has seized the public's attention in our own day. At least, in the case of Altizer, we must observe that the second possible meaning *alone* is insufficient. To the influence of Nietzsche (seen in the second possibility), we must add the mysticism of Luther (seen in the ninth possibility). It was in one of Luther's hymns that Nietzsche himself first came across the phrase "God is dead." [24] And, of course, Luther meant that, mystically, mysteriously, when Jesus died on the cross, God also died. This certainly is the interpretation that Altizer is currently giving to his position, and we must suspect that Hamilton is at least in sympathy with it, or he would not cooperate with Altizer on the writing of a book.[25]

It must be concluded, then, that the troubled Nietzsche, so ill-oriented to the culture of his own day, and so outstandingly radical in his rejection and reassessment of Western culture, has proven to be one of the most dynamic influences on the current situation in religious thought. But Nietzsche's influence runs wider and deeper than its effect on the radical theologians. Nietzsche is influential on much of the existentialist philosophy of our century because he represents a type of thought and interest that has sought and received its due importance in our era. This importance was often neglected in the nineteenth century, the century of the philosophical system and of the biological system of classification (Darwin). Nietzsche, along with the thinker we turn to next, represented the assertion of the defiant will and the honest mind which recognizes the unconquerable, irreducible element of the irrational — the antirational — in the world. The thinker who shared this vision of the unconquerable element of passion, of emotion, of subjectivity, of novelty in the cosmos was Søren Kierkegaard.

Søren Kierkegaard: The Attack on Christendom and the Residual Shock to Western Philosophy

Most of the men whom we have treated in this discussion of the negative or contrapuntal tradition in Western culture have placed their confidence in reason. Notable exceptions to this observation are Luther, who once salaciously referred to reason as " the devil's whore " (in his arguments with Erasmus), and Nietzsche. In Luther, the consequences of antirationalism were not worked out, except in reference to the Reformation religious principle of salvation by faith alone. Luther was no philosopher, although, like anyone else, he had his philosophic presuppositions and indeed had a relatively thorough understanding of scholastic dialectic. In Nietzsche, the irrational came to expression, not as the merely unknown aspect of the universe, or as an expression of the residual mysteries of life that plague man after all his theorizing, but as a viable alternative way of looking at the world. Zarathustra sings, in Nietzsche's vision:

I walk among men as the fragments of the future: that future which I contemplate. . . .
To redeem what is past, and to transform every " It was " into " Thus would I have it! " that only do I call redemption.[26]

Nietzsche's message was that *the will to live is the will to power,* and that no amount of moralizing and rationalizing (as in Kant's categorical imperative) can curb *man's will to be and to conquer* forever.

Since the will to power is an emotion, belonging to the human subject, Nietzsche represents a shift of interest in philosophic thought from the objective (the structures of the universe) to the subjective (the nature of the person with his needs and passions). Although there was no intercourse between them, both Nietzsche and Kierkegaard expressed the significance of human subjectivity. In the work of both men, we find a questioning of Western culture's overvaluation of

reason and the rational. Twentieth-century existentialist theology and philosophy — both Karl Barth and Jean-Paul Sartre,
despite their different visions — have founded themselves on
Nietzsche and Kierkegaard.

The thought world of Søren Kierkegaard, despite its common subjectivity with Nietzsche, is far different from that of
Zarathustra's creator. Kierkegaard was radical through and
through, and would violently attack the institution of the
church, but Kierkegaard never doubted the "reality" of God.

Søren Aabye Kierkegaard was born in 1813 and died in
1855. His life story is a classic one of the rebel who fought to
the death, whose ideals were rejected in his lifetime, and who
was to be accorded by history a delayed intellectual resurrection
so that, like Thomas à Becket, he could rule from the grave.
It would be a truism to say that Søren Kierkegaard exercised
no influence on the nineteenth century (his own), and that,
contrariwise, he has influenced the twentieth century beyond
all calculation. Kierkegaard was philosophy's ugly duckling,
who was not, however, seen to be a swan for some sixty years
after his demise. There were a few free thinkers — like Georg
Brandes, a Jewish thinker — who were attracted to Kierkegaard, but for the most part even Brandes' character sketch of
Kierkegaard in German in 1879 [27] was ignored. The rejection
of Kierkegaard by his age was due not only to his peculiar
style of life and his unpopular opinions but also to the fact
that he was — like the ugly duckling — a very strange duck
(philosopher) for his time. Kierkegaard swam directly opposite to the stream of thought that flowed from the water-
sheds of the wise in the mid-nineteenth century. He was a
radical's radical.

The thought world of Continental philosophy in Søren
Kierkegaard's era was dominated by the rational religious system of Georg Wilhelm Friedrich Hegel (1770–1831). Hegel
had conceived of God as the world process, or, in other terms,
of history as the unfolding life of God. And, in good Lutheran

Protestant fashion, Hegel came to the insight that the life of God was advancing in a threefold way. In other words, the world spirit (Hegel's term) was triune. Hegel, of course, might never have gotten off the ground with this idea if he had been reared a Unitarian.

However, Hegel's trinity is a bit different from the Trinity of the Christian creeds. To Kierkegaard — and to many orthodox believers — Hegel had dissolved the mystery of the Holy Trinity into an abstract, and perhaps artificial, movement of history. Kierkegaard considered that all attempts at providing Christianity with a rational justification were fundamentally irreligious. This brought him into conflict with orthodox rational theology and with the philosophy of Hegel, for Hegelianism claimed to be Christianity rationalized. Kierkegaard's *Concluding Unscientific Postscript to the Philosophical Fragments* (1846) was an attack on Hegel's claim to have demonstrated that human history is an intelligible plan in which God's will is manifest. According to Kierkegaard, it is ridiculous for any human being to pretend to such knowledge, for he would have to be God to know what only God could know. Kierkegaard considered that a preoccupation with science and with objective thinking (" objectivity") betrayed a desire to remain a mere spectator and to shirk the necessity of choosing for oneself. It was in opposition to this attitude that he proclaimed that " truth is subjectivity."

Kierkegaard's most scornful words were reserved for the great Germanic thinkers who believed themselves capable of catching up the essence of life and its mysteries in a systematic philosophy. Søren Kierkegaard quite understood that a logical system is possible, but denied that a system of existence is possible, because the one who would cast the system is included within it himself. He wrote: " Naturally, one can do with Hegel's logical trinity what one can do with everything — namely utter it, with application to the simplest object, where it is true indeed but none the less ridiculous." [28]

Kierkegaard's response to the well-wrought philosophical and theological systems of his day (and to the "tamed" Christian citizenship of his fellow citizens) was to raise the question of individual existence and the demand for individual decision about (and faith in) Christ. Kierkegaard began this positive side of his work in *The Philosophical Fragments*,[29] and in the *Concluding Unscientific Postscript to the Philosophical Fragments*,[30] he rejected all the traditional arguments for the existence of God, for the immortality of the soul, and for the rationality of ethics. Rather, he based everything on the believer's faith and his subjective need. However, Kierkegaard felt that this faith, which he said came only when one had fallen into despair about one's own possibilities, was a miraculous gift of God. Kierkegaard liked to use the analogy of learning to swim to describe his view of faith:

If one were to say that to swim is to lie upon dry land and squirm, every one would regard him as mad. But to believe is exactly like swimming, and instead of helping a man to get his feet on land, the preacher should help him to get out into the deep. So if one were to say that to believe is to lie upon dry land and go through the motions, all the time sure of the result, he is really saying the same thing as the above, only people perhaps do not notice it. . . . For a finite being — and surely that is what man is so long as he lives in the temporal sphere . . . — the negative infinity is the highest attainable, and the positive is a very questionable reassurance. Spiritual existence, and the religious existence in particular, is by no means easy; the believer lies constantly out upon the deep, with 70,000 fathoms of water under him. Long as he may lie there, he gets no comfort from the expectation that little by little (because of accumulated proofs) he will find himself on land, stretched out at his ease. He may, indeed, become calmer, more accustomed, find a sense of security which enables him to take pleasure in fun and light-hearted merriment — but until the last instant he lies above a depth of 70,000 fathoms.[31]

Kierkegaard directed all his attention to answering the question, "What does it mean to be a Christian?" His first answer was that it was not necessarily to be a member of the state Lutheran Church of Denmark. Kierkegaard saw the established church as complacent and unmindful of the radicality of the gospel. He saw the church "deifying" itself by identifying the outward appearance of the church with the inward. He called this almost total loss of transcendence permanent rebellion against God. That fundamental misfortune of Christianity is Christendom, was Kierkegaard's observation.

Over against the established church, Kierkegaard placed the individual who stood before God — and who could only become a Christian by God's grace and the "leap of faith."

Only a man of iron will can become a Christian. For only he has a will that can be broken. But a man of iron will whose will is broken by the Unconditional, i.e., by God, is a Christian.[32]

Kierkegaard leveled a frontal attack on the established church and on the university professors, ministers, and bishops who undergirded it with reasoned treatises, learned sermons, and beautiful rituals. He attacked two men who represented the learned and ecclesiastical classes, Professor Martensen and Bishop Mynster. Both men were decent, intelligent, and devout. By hitting them, Kierkegaard showed that he wanted to reject and denounce radically that which holds the highest reputation in Christendom.

Kierkegaard is the very model of the radical whose sharp attacks upon the *status quo*, with all their lack of proportion, have become a kind of orthodoxy in the succeeding century. Of course, much of Kierkegaard's critique was justified, just as we have seen that much of the critique made by each of the previously discussed radicals was justified. Perhaps the clearest expression of what he saw wrong with the "Christendom" of his day is his statement: "Christendom came about as soon as emphasis was laid upon 'extension' at the cost of 'intensity.'"[33] The very idea of a Christian society was as abhorrent to Kierkegaard as was the idea of a theological system. Rather than continuing with the pious fiction of a Christian nation and civilization, Kierkegaard called for a stress on following Jesus, upon becoming a disciple, upon renunciation of comfort and success in this world. This renunciation, or becoming a disciple, is not a matter of pious religious exercises, but a new way of seeing oneself as related to God. " Renunciation is a higher relationship to God, it is really a love relationship." [34] And to have this relationship to God results in living in such a way that others may take one for a fool — a fool for Christ. This worldly assessment of the disciple issues in suffering, the one mark of a genuine Christian. Against this " foolish " extremism, the established church stands, offering, instead of suffering, a way of salvation through Baptism and Christian education. Kierkegaard despised and rejected the way of the church.

The professors and parsons live by presenting the sufferings of others, and that is regarded as religiousness, uncommonly deep religiousness even; for the religiousness of the congregation is nothing else but hearing this presented. A *charmante* religiousness, just as genuine as tea made with a bit of paper which once lay in a drawer beside another bit of paper which once had been used to wrap a few dried tea-leaves from which tea had already been made three times.[35]

Thus Kierkegaard criticized the comfortable Christian Church of Denmark and, by extension, the church throughout the nineteenth-century world. He attacked the Christianity of his day as being the epitome of human ideals, tolerance, kindness, scholarship, cooperation, bourgeois morality, and philistinism. Although he was a Christian in that the object of his faith was Jesus Christ, Kierkegaard was a radical thinker unlike any other Christian thinker of his times. In his plunge into the depths of what it means to be a Christian, with the concomitant rejection of the institutions of his times, Kierkegaard is a fellow radical with the culture critic, Nietzsche, and the society critic, Karl Marx. While Kierkegaard argued that God's

Kingdom is not of this world, Marx was identifying the Kingdom of God with the projected classless society in which all members of society would share equally in the wealth of the world. We now leave the spiritual radical and turn to the worldly radical whose works have shaken Western culture to its very foundations.

Karl Marx: Religion as the Repressive Instrument of the Upper Classes

Karl Marx (1818–1883) was born of German Jewish parents who converted to Christianity during his childhood. His university days were spent in Berlin, where Hegel's influence was still strong. Marx apparently held radical political opinions from his youth, for he was involved in the unsuccessful German revolution of 1848, and was exiled for life at age thirty-one. Marx spent the balance of his life in England, earning his living as a newspaper correspondent. Living in London, working in the afternoons in the calm of the British Museum, Karl Marx set down on paper a group of radical theories that were destined to shatter the national and social fabric of the world.

Marx was influenced by the tremendous prestige that the natural sciences received during his lifetime. But he was even more influenced by the abject poverty and lack of social power of the working classes in Europe. Marx was moved to a powerful hatred of the landed gentry and merchant classes, because of the hopelessness and misery he saw in German and English slums. Like Comte, Marx felt a deep devotion to humanity, and had an entirely naturalistic understanding of the world. Under the driving force of his demand for social reform, and the influence of Comte, Hegel, and the naturalistic strand of European thought (such as Feuerbach), Marx produced a new philosophy.

Marx's view of the world is not a metaphysical one in the usual sense of that word. Rather, Marx thought of the world as the product of material forces at work in history. He offered

mankind an explanation (he claimed) of the nature of the social process that would provide the basis for enlightened social
action. History's processes, according to Marx's theory, are not
rational, but they do manifest a pattern of the inner play of
opposing and cooperating forces. Like Hegel, Marx saw these
historical processes as forces coming to consciousness in the
human race. *The Communist Manifesto* [36] opens with a declaration of Marx's radical insight, which was literally to turn
one third of the earth upside down in the twentieth century:
" The history of all hitherto existing society is the history of
class struggles." [37]

Marx, and his associate and philosophical heir, Engels, offered an absolutistic world view that saw the explanation for
and the foundations of every political, religious, and philosophical idea in " the prevailing mode of economic production
and exchange, and the social organization necessary following from it." [38]

According to Marx's materialistic conception of history, the
determining element in history is ultimately the production
and reproduction of real life through the economic processes
whereby man creates the commodities by which he lives. The
course of world history is not directed by ideas, but new ideas
are brought about by new means of production. The art,
literature, government, philosophy, and religion of any culture
are produced as a kind of ideological ("idea-system") super-
structure by the means by which men wrest their livelihood
from the earth. This idea-superstructure is unconsciously (and
sometimes consciously) created to serve the class of people
who control the means of production, e.g., the landowning
aristocrats in feudalism and the capitalists in nineteenth-
century Europe and America. Thus religion is seen by Marx
(and also Engels and later Lenin) as " the opiate of the people," i.e., of the proletariat, the oppressed working people.
The controlling classes inculcate religious hopes and fears in
the proletariat in order to keep them subservient to their in-

terests. Religion teaches that men should not kill, or steal, or disobey rulers; thus it contributes to the stability of the *status quo*, and keeps the workers docile so that the rich may continue to exploit them. God is but the projected figure of the ruler, a type of king or prime minister whom no one can assassinate, whom no one can deceive. Religion's preaching about the Kingdom of God or heaven also serves the ruling classes, Marx said, because by holding out the promise of " pie in the sky by and by," the workers are made more willing to suffer injustice in this life.

What can we say to such an indictment of religion? For Marx's " explanation " is not really the result of a scientific observation of the whole range of religious phenomena; rather, it is a searchingly radical indictment, a too-often true indictment, of man's misuse of the religious impulse. It cannot be denied that too many times religious faith is used to preserve a *status quo*. It cannot be denied that too often the church has let itself be used as a bulwark of the ruling classes in exchange for the support of those groups. The " inner missions " and " industrial missions " of the twentieth century bear witness to the truth that lies behind Marx's attack on the organized Christianity of nineteenth-century Europe. Like Kierkegaard, Marx overreacted, but it is the element of truth in Marx's overreaction that makes Marxism a persistent opponent of Christianity in the twentieth century.

We are not concerned to trace the intricacies of the Marxian dialectic here, for that has been done from several different viewpoints in books available to everyone.[39] What we are concerned about is the radical stance that Marx and Engels took toward the world of their time. Although Marxist theory was, and still is, an oversimplification of the historical (social) process, there are large elements of truth in his vision that have passed out of the hands of doctrinaire Marxists and even of the more intelligent and democratic socialists, to become part of the world view of our own times. To accept Marx's analysis of history as an economically determined process of struggle between social classes is to sacrifice one's intellect and integrity, for history is obviously more than this one strand. But, to reject all of Marx's insights in the name of some equally abstract construct of beliefs like " capitalism " is to be equally dishonest with ourselves. Marx's constuctive ideas, the influence of economic conditions on the intellectual life of a period, the importance of great social groups in the formation of culture and beliefs, the scaling down of the importance of outstanding individuals like kings and philosophers, and the sense that history and culture are a unity into which all the varied elements of human life flow, ought to be, and largely have been, accepted by intelligent men. As with the other radicals we have surveyed, that which was good in Marx's message has been appropriated by modern man, and that which was not good (the emphasis on revolution, the oversimplification of religion, and intellectual life) has been rejected. Not even the Soviets live by an unadulterated Marx today, but not even the free world has escaped taking his criticisms seriously. History has a way of making omelets in which the best part of the broken eggs rises to the surface.

Sigmund Freud: Projection as the Explanation of the God Hypothesis

Sigmund Freud (1856–1939) was born of Jewish parents in Freiberg, Moravia, then part of Austria, and brought up in Vienna. He once said of himself, " My parents were Jews and I remained a Jew," although a biographer has written that Freud was a " natural atheist " all his life.[40] Essentially Freud thought of religion in terms of the deterministic naturalism hammered out in the nineteenth century by Darwin and other biological and social scientists (such as Comte). Religion represented an institutionalized illusion to Freud, the modern concentration of the fears and desires of primitive men who personified the forces of nature. Actually, the fears and psychic needs of the human being form the real contents of the projected gods and spirits. Even the lofty idea of God as the universal Father, Freud saw as the result of primitive attempts to deal with psychic fears and guilt feelings that derived from sex conflicts within human social groups.

Freud's conception of the rise of man's belief in a Father-God is well known and often damned as the rankest atheism. However, it remains quite influential on the thought world of our day and must be reassessed.

Basically, Freud resorts to the creation of a new mythology in order to explain the rise of the God hypothesis. That it is the production of Freud's fertile imagination and not a result of some anthropological investigation should be borne in mind.

Roughly speaking, Freud sees the God hypothesis as a resultant from the sexual conflict between children and their parents. In other words, belief in God comes about because of the Oedipus complex in man. The young child, according to Freud, experiences a sexual development early, in which the young boy's sexual feelings are directed toward his mother. This youthful desire for the mother is accompanied by jealousy of the father. However, the situation is not so simple as that — there is more involved than love for mother and hate for father. The boy has ambivalent feelings toward the father, hating him because he possesses the mother, but admiring him because of his size and strength, an admiration that may pass over into love and respect. Basically, the boy would be like his father (which he will be in time) and also take his place with the mother (which society's taboos prevent). This is Freud's unraveling of the Oedipus complex, so named because of the dramatic hero of ancient Greece who inadvertently killed his own father and married (and had children by) his own mother.

Freud projects this family conflict upon the whole of the human race, using this sexual conflict to explain human ideas about and attitudes toward God. In human prehistory, he

imagines, men roved the earth in small bands, made up of
one strong, older male (the dominant male noted in the study
of monkey hordes), who fathered all the younger members
of the group, and who reserved to himself all sexual rights with
the group's females. Freud called this "social organization"
the primal horde.[41]

Freud credits the theory of the primal horde to Charles
Darwin, although he offers some additions to it. "One day,"
Freud writes, "the expelled brothers [who had been driven
out of the horde when they made sexual advances to females
in the group] joined forces, slew and ate the father, and thus
put an end to the father horde. . . . This violent primal father
had surely been the envied and feared model for each of
the brothers. Now they accomplished their identification with
him by devouring him and each acquired a part of his strength.
The totem feast [analogous to the Passover meal and the
Lord's Supper], which is perhaps mankind's first celebration,
would be the repetition and commemoration of this mem-
orable, criminal act with which so many things began, social
organization, moral restrictions and religion." [42]

Freud remarks later: "After they had satisfied their hate by
his [the father's] removal and had carried out their wish for
identification with him, the suppressed tender impulses had
to assert themselves." [43]

The above passages from Freud's psychological works reveal the complete materialistic determinism that underlies his
system. As in the case of Marx, Freud recognized the existence of no other elements in the world but material ones;
hence he was unable to deal with religion or art or literature
in anything but a reductionistic way. Freud had to reduce everything he observed to the terms with which he was familiar.
In his case these terms were the psychology of sex. For this
reason, most intellectuals today would not accept as being
correct Freud's explanation of belief in God as projection.
However, the fact that there are elements of projection in the

psychology of religion has been recognized by psychologists, sociologists, and theologians. As in the case of Feuerbach, Freud put his finger on one of the psychic mechanisms involved in religion, and the truth of his insight has passed into the makeup of the modern world view. The weakness of Freud's theory is also the weakness of Marx's theory of history, that is, it is a new ideology and not a scientific description of the whole range of human experience.

Summary of the Critical Tradition in Western Culture

The problem arises in each of these representatives of the negative or contrapuntal tradition as to how we are to deal with the more than material aspects of man. For the ancient critics, Xenophanes, Socrates, the Cynics, etc., there was no problem of dealing with the human spirit. Each of these representatives was actually fighting for the spiritual over against the material evaluation of man. However, even in ancient times there was a more caustic variety of criticism. This hard core of radical thought is best seen in Epicurus, the famous philosopher who founded the Epicurean school in order to free men from the fear and anxiety caused them by beliefs in the gods. Epicurus felt that belief in the divine undercut man's peace of mind, so he taught that although there may be divine beings (since men saw such gods in their dreams), these divine beings were interested in their own affairs and certainly were not sufficiently concerned with what the weak race of men did to interfere in their lives. Thus Epicurus taught that men ought to forget about the gods. As to the fear of death, which plagues mankind, Epicurus saw this too as the result of belief in gods who would punish men in an afterlife for their deeds on earth. Epicurus counseled indifference to this fear also, because "where you are death is not, and where death is you are not." In other words, there is no life beyond death, and this situation should not cause men concern, for they will not exist to be troubled by their own death.

Epicurus was followed two centuries later by a Latin disciple, Lucretius, who set Epicurus' practical atheism in verse, writing a long poem, "On the Nature of Things." Lucretius also viewed the deity as mankind's greatest disturber and counseled that men should live as if there were no gods.

We find such hard-core radical thought even in the Old Testament, particularly in the book called Ecclesiastes. Despite the attempts of the more orthodox Hebrew editors, the essential message of Ecclesiastes comes across plainly: Human life is vain and ultimately meaningless.

> Vanity of vanities, says the Preacher,
> vanity of vanities! All is vanity.
> What does man gain by all the toil
> at which he toils under the sun?
> A generation goes, and a generation comes,
> but the earth remains for ever.
> (Eccl. 1:2-4.)

What is remarkable about the critical radicals of later times, as we have discussed them above, is that, with the exception of Luther and Kierkegaard, the radicals since the Reformation have been of the severely or hard-core negative type. In Comte and Feuerbach, we have the doctrines of religion explained purely naturally. In Nietzsche, we have the announcement of "the death of God," who has been killed by modern man's scientific advancement and control of nature. In Marx and Freud, we again find a purely natural explanation of religion, but with the added criticism that sees religion as an illusion that should be surpassed. Only Luther and Kierkegaard escape the trap of positivism and its sisters and brothers among the materialistic evaluations of the universe. Thus the radical of modern times leaves us with the problem of how to deal with those aspects of our experience which we cannot in good conscience explain away as the effects of material forces. We are, we find, left with more problems that demand solutions, when we adopt a materialistic outlook, than we had when we held to an outlook that admitted the action of spirit in a world of matter. Two prominent thinkers of our century, Julian Huxley [44] and Alfred North Whitehead,[45] have discussed this aspect of mankind's adoption of a materially oriented world view, and have declared that there is an inner demand in the human reason for mysticism. By mysticism, both men seem to mean that man needs a sense of unity with his fellows and of unity with the universe itself. Immanuel Kant (1724–1804), often called the first modern philosopher, without an understanding of whom one cannot understand modern philosophy, also concluded that man's commitment to coherence demands a sense of the unity of the ideas in his mind and the events that take place in the world. Kant interpreted this demand of the practical reason to mean that we must posit a unity of the soul and the " ideal of pure reason " (or God) that unites subject and object, in the unity of a universe. Kant was well aware that he could not establish the existence of a God or, for that matter, the existence of a self or of a universe on the basis of his critical philosophy, but he also recognized that the acceptance of self, God, and universe were practical necessities of human life. In his famous discussion of the antinomies, Kant shows that the universe both implies and does not imply the existence of God. Kant and the people of his day were willing, under those circumstances, to assume that there was a God. However, in the 150 years since Kant, the willingness to make this assumption has been largely swept away. Nietzsche, writing at the end of the nineteenth century, makes just the opposite assumption from that of Kant, and declares that God is dead. In a sense, the recent radical crisis in theology is a delayed reaction to the growing understanding of modern man that the elements that make up our world view have made it impossible for us to follow Kant and apparently make it necessary to accept Nietzsche. Thus, the problem today is, How is theology possible in a time that recognizes that its world view has no place for God?

Chapter II
Critical Scholarship and Rationalistic Orthodoxy [1]

IT MAY SEEM strange to begin a discussion of the current "death of God" movement in the sixth century B.C., as we did in Chapter I, when we began our study of the critical tradition with Thales and the ancient Greek philosophers, but the truth is that if we would understand the contrapuntal tradition which is emerging as a major force in our day, we must start at the very beginning of Western civilization. The reasoning behind this statement is this: Throughout Western man's twenty-six-hundred-year philosophical development, there have been at least two major streams of tradition. The one stream we may call the orthodox, or the positive, tradition, which we may identify with Plato and Aristotle in the pre-Christian period, along with the positive evaluation of the Greek myths in Homer, and after the rise of Christianity, the tradition that runs through Irenaeus, Athanasius, and Augustine. This orthodox or Catholic tradition becomes fixed and regulated in the period known as the early Middle Ages, and is cast in the form of systematic theological statements during the high Middle Ages. The orthodox or Catholic tradition thus comes to its clearest expression in the works of Thomas Aquinas. As we know, only a century and a half was to elapse before the great construct of the medieval Catholic tradition was challenged by the pre-Reformation heresies, such as the Waldensians. Soon John Hus was to challenge the orthodox

tradition which the councils of the Catholic Church had identified with the truth of the Christian religion. However, in the
Hussite movement of Bohemia as well as in the movements
begun by Peter Waldo in France and Italy and John Wycliffe,
in England, the essential points of the orthodox tradition remained unchallenged. The differences between the various
pre-Reformation movements and the Catholic Church were
differences of interpretation and not differences of belief in
the substance of the classical and Christian foundations of the
medieval world view.

The sixteenth century saw an even more profound shock to
the orthodox or Catholic tradition with the rise of Luther
and the German Anabaptist Reformers. However, in Luther, all
the essential elements of the orthodox Catholic tradition were
reaffirmed, and indeed belief in the substance of that tradition
was intensified. In a similar manner, the Anabaptists also laid
claim to a more devout belief in the substance of the orthodox
tradition by stressing the immanence of the Divine and re-
stricting the scope of the doctrines they considered necessary
for salvation. We might observe, therefore, that the Protestant
Reformation, in all its aspects, did nothing to change the essential nature of the orthodox tradition, although in the event it
was to weaken it by splitting the monolithic unity of the Christian world. However, the orthodox tradition was given one of
its most uncompromising expressions by one of the second-
generation leaders of the Reformation, the father of Protestant
systematic theology, John Calvin.

The other wing of the orthodox tradition showed itself in-
capable of taking the criticisms of the Protestant revolt within
itself and satisfying its demand, by unilaterally restating and
fixing the elements of the orthodox tradition in the decrees
of the Council of Trent (1545–1563). The Roman Catholic
Church, for such was a true description of the church that
held to the formula of Trent, established itself upon the in-
errancy of the Scriptures and tradition of the ancient Catho-

lic Church, and on the decisions of the great synods and the pronouncements of the popes.

Thus, at the end of the sixteenth century, we have the phenomena of the orthodox tradition having undergone a process of cellular division that resulted in two similar bodies, each claiming to possess the true knowledge of God, man, and the world.

The orthodox Catholic tradition was never the full story of the philosophical and theological development of the West, however. In fact, the orthodox tradition was hammered out by a process of definition of the " correct " view of God, man, and the world in a series of struggles with representatives of other interpretations of the classical and Christian inheritance. Indeed, it is truthful to say that almost no element of the orthodox tradition of the West emerged without this process of testing and refinement through opposition. In philosophy, the view of the universe as rational (one might call it the Apollinarian tradition, as Nietzsche does [2]) was opposed from the beginnings of Western culture by the mythological, demonic view that saw the world as the product of divine (and irrational) forces. Plato's belief in the immortality of the soul, which became a solid part of the orthodox Western tradition, had its opposition in Aristotle's philosophy — which, shorn of its " heresy," itself became a large part of the Western tradition. In theology, the process of " indirect progress " by assertion and refutation is even clearer. Every one of the statements in the Nicene Creed and the Athanasian Creed was hammered out in this way. Arius versus Athanasius over the person of Christ; Apollinarius versus Athanasius over the natures of Christ; Nestorius versus Cyril over the humanity of Christ; Eutyches versus Cyril and Leo over the divinity of Christ. Without the " heretics " to keep them honest, the " orthodox " theologians would never have come to the fullest understanding of what they meant when they confessed, " Jesus is Lord."

It is this critical, antithetical tradition, often standing under the anathema of the church and the disdain of the academy that we have designated the contrapuntal tradition. It forms "the other" that is essential to the self-identity of the orthodox tradition throughout the classical Greek, primitive Christian, "Dark," and Middle Ages of Western culture.

We ought to be clear about the meaning of "heresy" in this regard. The word "heresy" is derived from a Greek root meaning "choice." It is the election of another option, of another interpretation. At its strongest use, i.e., in its use to mean "false" doctrine, it means no more than "bad theology." It does not have to mean "bad religion," for religion and theology are not the same. Religion is one's belief in the Ultimate (usually called "God") and one's effort to live by one's beliefs. Theology, on the other hand, is a systematic, rational presentation (and explanation) of what the religious community believes. Theology is the "science" of religion. One can "have religion" in the best sense and be "heretical," i.e., give a different interpretation of what the community believes than the official representatives of that community may give. Unfortunately, this distinction works in reverse too. It is perfectly possible to present a "good" (i.e., accepted, orthodox) theology, and have little or no religion. In that case one looks upon the religion in question in the way that a philosopher may look upon a philosophical system which he does not personally accept. Or, unfortunately, one may pretend a concern for and loyalty to the religion and in actuality by a hypocrite. One's orthodoxy or lack of it is no guarantee that one is or is not "faithful," however. True religion has always been considered to be more than the acceptance of a catechism or creed.

The breaking point in the orthodox Western tradition, as we have noted above, is not the Reformation — indeed, it is not found in an event of the church's history at all. Rather, the breaking point, the "hinge" of our particular cultural history, which includes the church, is found in the secular experience of the *Aufklärung*, or the Enlightenment, and its change of the direction of human thought.

We are not concerned here with the major figures of the philosophic Enlightenment — John Locke, Bishop Berkeley, Voltaire, David Hume, Condillac, Hamann, Thomas Reid, Lichtenberg — but with the men who followed them in the late eighteenth and early nineteenth centuries. It was by these thinkers, the philosopher Immanuel Kant (1724–1804) and the theologian Friedrich Schleiermacher (1768–1834), that the orthodox tradition was examined (in the most sympathetic way) and found wanting. In a very real sense, Kant forms the "watershed" of the stream of philosophy, giving the major direction of its flow since his time, and Schleiermacher stands as the "Kant" of modern theology. After a brief discussion of what Kant and Schleiermacher did to bring the Western tradition to grips with the reality of the "modern" world, we shall turn to an analysis of how critical scholarship contributed to the breakup of the orthodox tradition. Chapter III will then tell the story of how "the great synthesizers" of the recent scholarly world tried to salvage as much of orthodoxy as was possible. Chaper IV will relate why this noble attempt has failed and produced an era that is aware of "the death of God."

Kant: The Separation of the Pure (Scientific) Reason from the Practical (Religious) Reason

Immanuel Kant was reared in the great pietistic tradition of German Protestantism, and although his religious outlook was to become very sophisticated indeed, he never lost that strong sense of duty and of responsibility for others that grew out of the resoluteness of the Germanic character (although his ancestors were Scotch!) and the influence of the Golden Rule on the pious peasant classes. Late in his life, when he wrote *Religion Within the Limits of Reason Alone*, Kant was to give voice to this sense of moral obligation in clear tones:

Whatever, over and above good life-conduct, man fancies that he can do to become well-pleasing to God is mere religious illusion and pseudo-service of God.[3]

Kant, in his analysis of the orthodox Western Christian tradition, did not proceed to rationalize (i.e., philosophize) Christianity, as was later the case with Georg W. F. Hegel (1770–1831). Kant was prevented from accepting rationalism completely by the influence on his thought of David Hume and John Locke, both of whom presented a basic skepticism concerning human reason. Kant once said that reading Hume had awakened him from the mental "sleep" of rationalism.

Because of his "critical" approach to all problems, philosophical and theological, Kant proceeded to base his religious teachings on a denial of the traditional, orthodox, and rationalistic philosophical "proofs" of the existence of God. In his *Critique of Pure Reason*,[4] Kant carefully overturned the ontological, cosmological, and teleological proofs of God's existence, but denied that he did not believe in God. What Kant actually accomplished was the demonstration that man can have no knowledge of God, which is similar to the theological position of Karl Barth in the twentieth century. Kant's purpose, too, was similar to Barth's, for he declared: "I have found it necessary to deny knowledge, in order to make room for faith."

Essentially, Kant separated religion (and ethics) from the domain of reason in the strict sense of "pure reason." Kant denied that we have knowledge about God, the soul, eternal rewards, and punishments, spirits, sin, etc., in the usual sense of the word "knowledge." "Knowledge" is restricted to what man can observe and generalize about, what man can weigh and judge and cast in the forms of "natural law." Religion, after Kant, can no longer claim to be supported by reason or proofs. As Kant said, he demolished knowledge in religion to make room for the true vehicle of religious conviction, faith. Kant asserted that all religious propositions (and ethical ones as well) were synthetic judgments. This means that religious affirmations do not describe (analyze) what we experience, but add to experience something not " given " in it or that is necessarily implied in it. Knowledge, however, in the sphere of pure or " scientific " reason, is the result of analytic judgments which describe the contents of experience and which can be judged true or false by reference back to the original things or experience in question. Religious judgments have no such " check." They can be judged only by the law of contradiction, which asks, " Does this judgment contradict the original experience, thing, or concept? " Even the law of contradiction cannot " prove " such a synthetic judgment true, however; only the conformity of this judgment to the widest and most inclusive contents of our human experience can do that. Kant felt that such conformity to experience was certainly possible in the case of ethical or value judgments. To cover these larger, socially valuable aspects of the human judgment, Kant projected another sphere, " The Practical Reason."

Kant is well known for his moralism, since he, more than any other modern philosopher, underscored the feeling of obligation, the awareness of " the categorical imperative " in the human being. By establishing the necessity of ethics, Kant felt that he had laid the practical foundation to reintroduce religion and make possible belief in the God whose existence the orthodox tradition, taken as a system of reasoning, was not able to establish. Kant overturned the older " proofs " of God, only to offer a new one, the moral argument for God's existence. In his *Critique of Practical Reason*, Kant declared:

Two things fill the mind with ever new and increasing admiration and awe, the oftener and more steadily we reflect on them: the starry heavens above me and the moral law within me.[5]

Kant deduced the moral law from his profound belief in human freedom. He felt that because we feel free, we therefore feel responsible. To be conscious of our freedom of choice in action is to be impressed with a sense of moral obligation to act constructively. And there is more than " feeling " here, there is definitely a logical possibility that we are just what we feel ourselves to be. In any event, the experience that we act as if we were free and accomplish (many times) the intention of our action bears out the reality of human freedom. We are not conscious of being determined, but we are conscious of deciding for ourselves. The practical reason acts on this consciousness.

But what is the content of this moral law? It is the sense of oughtness that leads us to so act that the basis of our action could become a universal law. Kant writes:

Ask yourself whether, if the action you propose should take place by a law of nature of which you yourself were a part, you could regard it as possible through your will.[6]

In other words, we are to conduct ourselves toward others according to the moral law, in ways that we would not mind having applied to ourselves. " Do unto others as you would have them do unto you."

The acceptance of the moral law makes it possible, and even necessary, says Kant, to believe in God through faith. Belief in God serves to strengthen our practical moral life. God is a necessity of the practical reason, for we can never attain the highest good if there is no God, who by definition is man's highest good. Thus faith posits God's existence:

Faith is assent on grounds that are subjectively sufficient in spite of being objectively insufficient.[7]

In the final analysis, belief in God is introduced in his system and allowed by Kant in order to fortify the moral sense within human beings. The God of the " First Cause " of Aristotle did not exist in Kant's judgment. Neither did the God who Anselm (A.D. 1033–1109) said was " a being than which nothing greater can be conceived." [8] Nor did the creator of the universe, spoken of by Plato in the Timaeus and the Hebrew sages in

Genesis, exist. In the *Critique of Practical Reason,* Kant declared that the question of who made us has no bearing on our feeling of freedom, which, being the basis of the moral law, is also the basis of Kant's view of religion. The concept of God would certainly be much modified in philosophy and theology after Kant. With religion subsumed under morality, and morality made the *sine qua non* for the positing of God's existence, the contrapuntal tradition had triumphed. Reason could no longer be used as a prop for piety, and faith could no longer be assent to intellectually perceived propositions. A new relationship between mind and spirit would have to be forged. The orthodox tradition was now viable only for those who, in Hegel's words, "have not yet reached the Kantian standpoint."[9] But Friedrich Ernst Daniel Schleiermacher (1768–1834) knew his Kant, and modified theology accordingly. To Schleiermacher we now turn.

Schleiermacher: The Contents of the Christian Faith Are Drawn from the Religious Consciousness (which is a modification of feeling) Alone

The young Schleiermacher was a "boundary-type" personality, on the order of the famous twentieth-century theologian Paul Tillich.[10] Essentially, Schleiermacher developed theology in the direction of a science of the (Kantian) practical reason.

In his early work *On Religion: Speeches to Its Cultured Despisers,*[11] Schleiermacher disassociated religion and piety from knowledge.[12] Like Kant, he sought out a different sphere for the religious life, but for Schleiermacher it was less the practical (or active) life than in Kant. For Schleiermacher, the sphere of religion is contemplation.[13]

The contemplation of the pious is the immediate consciousness of the universal existence of all finite things, in and through the Infinite, and of all temporal things in and through the

Eternal. . . . It is to have life and to know life in immediate feeling.[14]

Thus Schleiermacher "staked out" an area for the religious life that was exempt (up to this time) from the inroads of critical philosophy and the growing branches of science. In his great *Glaubenslehre*, or dogmatics,[15] written in 1821–1822 (revised in 1830), Schleiermacher claimed to present the Christian faith systematically, according to the fundamental doctrines of the Evangelical (i.e., Lutheran and Reformed) Church. Schleiermacher does make such a dogmatic presentation, but within this significant framework:

The piety which forms the basis of all ecclesiastical communions is, considered purely in itself, neither a knowing nor a doing, but a modification of feeling, or of immediate self-consciousness.[16]

Schleiermacher gives an interesting discussion of knowing, doing, and feeling, and elects feeling as the basic state of man's immediate self-consciousness. "Feeling is the one to which piety belongs,"[17] Schleiermacher declares, for:

The common element in . . . expressions of piety, . . . the self-identical essence of piety, is this: the consciousness of being absolutely dependent, or, which is the same thing, of being in relation with God.[18]

This famous definition of piety, as absolute (German *schlechthinig*) dependence upon God, is, of course, directly contradictory of Kant's belief in man's absolute freedom. In fact, Schleiermacher says directly: "There can . . . be for us no such thing as a feeling of absolute freedom."[19] Schleiermacher seems to have a better argument than Kant, in that Schleiermacher clearly demonstrates that every feeling of freedom has a feeling of limitation in it also. It would be possible to speak of being absolutely free only if "the object (of our attention) altogether came into existence through our activity, which is never the case absolutely, but only relatively."[20]

Actually, man is aware both of feelings of relative (or limited) freedom and of absolute dependence upon God — who is not identical with the world or any part of it (for the world does not move us to absolutes).[21] This is an interesting development in Schleiermacher, for in *On Religion*,[22] Schleiermacher pretty clearly identified God and the world.

Is not God the highest, the only unity? Is it not God alone before whom and in whom all particular things disappear? And if you see the world as a whole, a Universe, can you do it otherwise than in God? . . . Otherwise than by the emotions produced in us by the world we do not claim to have God in our feeling, and consequently I have not said more of Him.[23]

Although this may be called pantheism by those who like to label people, it is certainly a set of insights about the Divine that must be included in any description of the Divine and our relation to it. Schleiermacher apparently moved his position from this " divinity of the whole " position to one that spoke of the Divine as omnipresent in the sense that God transcends the universe in which he is also immanent.[24] However, Schleiermacher's identification of God in *The Christian Faith,* though more developed, is actually less definite than his mystical affirmations in *On Religion.*

In Volume I of *The Christian Faith,* Schleiermacher simply says: " In the first instance God signifies for us simply that which is the co-determinant in this feeling and to which we trace our being in such a state; and any further content of the idea must be evolved out of this fundamental import assigned to it." [25] In other words, " God-consciousness " is caused by something we will designate as " God," but this God-consciousness is included within human self-consciousness and cannot be separated from it. God, thus, " is given to us in feeling in an original way," and only in this way.[26] To speak of God as anything else than the constitutive element in our feeling of dependence is to speak symbolically or corruptly (idolatrously).[27] Surely this manner of speaking of God, for all its sophistication and piety, is less moving and spiritually viable than the near-pantheism of Schleiermacher's earlier work. Although Schleiermacher disagreed with Kant over the nature of human freedom, and consequently built his theological exposition in a different fashion than Kant, both accomplished the same result. Kant effectively separated pure or worldly reason from practical (ethical and spiritual) reason, thus precluding the possibility of speaking of knowledge of God or knowledge of ethics. Schleiermacher, by drawing the contents of the Christian faith exclusively from the religious self-consciousness or the immediate self-consciousness of man which senses an absolute dependence upon stronger forces (God), effectively removed theology from the noetic world of "real" (material and perceptive) things. With "faith" defined as "feeling," and "God" defined as what "causes" this feeling, the philosophical and theological question of the ontological (reality) status of the referent (if any) of this "feeling" is simply abandoned. Schleiermacher's theology was a grand tour de force which rejected any attempt to involve Christianity on the phenomenological (event, experience, fact) level of reality. In Kant's famous terms, religion, for Schleiermacher resides in the noumena (the structures of the mind), and we can say nothing about its relation (if any) to the phenomenal (experienced) world of materiality.

In terms of the phenomenal world of gravity, weight, force, mass, and blood pressure, already in the year 1830, there was no God to trouble oneself with. Tacitly in Schleiermacher's case, and overtly in the earlier case of Kant, a stamp of approval was put on Laplace's remark to Napoleon concerning God, which ran: "I have no need of that hypothesis."

The Contrapuntal Tradition Displaces the Orthodox Tradition: The Rise of Liberal Religious Thought

Between 1830 (the appearance of Schleiermacher's dogmatics) and the 1890's [28] a number of developments that had been at work since the mid-eighteenth century came to full fruition.

There were at least four major streams of the liberal tradition that progressed toward the absolute polarization of Christian thinkers and believers in general into two schools. These streams or elements in the contrapuntal tradition are:

1. The rise of modern Biblical scholarship, and the consequent change of place of the Bible in Western thought.

2. The rise of the " history of religions " school, in which the beliefs of the Bible were identified as related to other religions both primitive and modern.

3. The struggle between the fundamentalists (or Bible literalists) and the promoters of the theory of evolution. The right wing decided to fight over a literal interpretation of the Creation story in Genesis. The "evolutionists" obliged them by fighting back. The philologists and classicists got into the struggle also. The upshot of all this was that most of the contents of the Bible was identified as religious myth and legend.

4. The quest from the very beginning of the modern (liberal) study of the Bible, for the essential facts about Jesus of Nazareth. This quest for " the historical Jesus " [29] as distinct from " the Christ of Faith " [30] ultimately failed. The content of liberal, " Jesus-centered " piety evaporated under the heat of critical scholarship.

Let us investigate how these streams passed over the watershed of Kant and Schleiermacher and passed through the gorges of orthodoxy, to flow, finally and freely, into the ocean of modern historical self-understanding.

The Rise of Modern Biblical Scholarship

Nowhere else can we see the struggle between the orthodox Christian tradition, with its utter literalistic belief in the sources of the Western tradition, and the contrapuntal tradition, with its stress on a critical handling of the elements of our tradition, than in the struggles that attended the rise of modern Biblical scholarship.

The orthodox tradition, as we have suggested above, embraced both the Roman Catholic and the Protestant communions, and at the beginning of this period of critical study, embraced the Jewish synagogue also.[31]

Briefly put, the orthodox Biblicism embraced these elements: The sacred writings of the Old and New Testaments were believed to be divinely inspired in the literal sense that God either dictated the words to the writers of these documents or at least, suggested the contents and the phrasing " by His Spirit." These sacred writings are thus all of a piece — each segment being as fully inspired as any other piece, no distinctions being permitted between the " histories " of the Chronicles and the words of Jesus in the New Testament. The orthodox theologians even held that the vowel points of the Hebrew text were inspired by God — even though these were not added until the years A.D. 1000–1200 by the Jews of Spain! All parts of the sacred text were thought of as one inseparable mass, all of which must be accepted as literally true on pain of excommunication and damnation. The various types of materials in the Bible, for the writings made up a " Bible " singular — and not a group of documents — were not theologically distinguished. Jonah's sojourn in the " great fish " was not thought to be of any different quality from Jesus' teachings about love of neighbor. No part of the Bible was recognized as legend or myth.

Of course, beliefs like these made a set of casuistic hermeneutical (interpretative) principles necessary. Thus, theologians looked for mystical meanings in the " numbers " of the book of Revelation, and found " morals " for the sensibilities of more sensitive ages in the bloodthirsty events of the Old Testament. One chief interpretative principle of the orthodox was the belief that everything in the Bible was absolutely unique. The Hebrews were not thought to have learned anything from the Egyptians or Chaldeans. Jesus was said to be unique in his message, no connection being seen between Jesus and the Jewish rabbinical tradition. Even the language of Scripture was thought to be unique. Hebrew was said to be the original language of Adam, and the New Testament was said to have been written in " sacred Greek."

Views like the above naturally made the orthodox the enemies of scientific research, most especially when such research made it clear that Hebrew was not the " original " language, and showed that the Egyptian civilization had existed for thousands of years before the date the orthodox claimed to be the day of Creation! As history, archaeology, philology, geology, etc., gradually showed the dependence of the Old Testament on its Middle Eastern environment, and revealed the fact that the Scriptures had naturally evolved in history like anything else, the war of the orthodox versus the liberals broke out with full fury.

The orthodox tradition was utterly rationalistic in its method of teaching and interpretation, but its contents were irrational. The liberal or contrapuntal tradition in this struggle over the Bible represented true rationality in that it sought knowledge of the genetic development of things and searched for underlying causation. The orthodox claimed to be defending " the truth," but used any means possible to fight their foes, fair or unfair. The liberals, by and large, were motivated with the desire to search for " truths." The orthodox could say with Tertullian, the fourth-century A.D. churchman, " I believe [the gospel] because it is absurd." The liberals formed the counterpoint to this by attempting to keep the belief while rejecting the absurdity. Few, if any, of the orthodox's worst enemies were atheists; most were Christians with a keener sense of truth than the masses.

Beginning with the Renaissance, scholars turned to the ancient documents of the West's classical and Christian tradition with a view to understanding them for what they were in themselves, instead of merely accepting the traditions about them handed down from the Middle Ages. The first of the great critical scholars was Lorenzo Valla, who proved that the documents which the Roman Catholic Church claimed gave the pope the same powers as were exercised by the Roman emperors were forgeries. Later, other scholars examined the text of the Old and New Testaments and found that the received texts of both testaments were in a state of delapidation because of uncritical additions made over the centuries. At first, men like Erasmus who tried to discover the original text of the Bible were subjected to church discipline. Such resistance to scholarly study was to go on until the third quarter of the nineteenth century among both Catholics and Protestants.

In the eighteenth century, however, the scholarly findings began to gain momentum, with the discovery that Hebrew was not the original language of man, with the discovery of the physician Astruc that the Pentateuch was made up of several strands of tradition, and last of all, with the discovery that the prophets formed the oldest strata of the Old Testament and the laws the newest. The orthodox theologians continued to oppose the findings of the scholars, but after about 1869, with the publication of *The Religion of Israel*,[32] by Kuenen, most of the thinking teachers of the church accepted the "higher criticism" as true. Throughout this whole period of scholarly discovery, conservatives of all communions continued to resist the evidence of the scholars and equated belief in Christ with a literal belief in the absurdities of the medieval tradition. This orthodox view has continued to our own day among a small group known as the fundamentalists.

The Rise of the "History of Religions" School

Along with the discoveries about the true nature of the original documents from ancient times, including the Scriptures, there was also a parallel study of the events of the ancient past by historians and archaeologists. These scholars, very early, demonstrated that it was absurd to date the Creation some four thousand years before Christ, as was done by the orthodox, for the high civilization of Egypt alone could be traced back five thousand years before Christ. Later scholars turned to the Mesopotamian civilizations, and discovered that civilization was even older than they had projected. They also discovered that the religion of the Old Testament was very similar to the older religions of Assyria and Babylonia. The orthodox were enraged to be told that the word "Sabbath," the story of the Flood, the story of Creation, and the story of the tower of Babel, had all been part of the earlier Chaldean religion. However, by the 1890's all scholarly theologians were forced to admit that these findings were true. Later studies such as those by Hatch [33] demonstrated the relationship of Christianity to the philosophy and religious ideas of the Greeks. The study known as the "history of religions" has grown more and more important as it has become more extensive in the twentieth century. Such outstanding scholars as Mircea Eliade [34] have turned to the investigation of primitive religions and the Far Eastern religions, finding much in them that is common in Christianity and Judaism. The fundamentalists of today continue to reject much of the "history of religions" material because of the danger they see in its acceptance to the uniqueness of their faith. However, the leading theologians of the church make use of the "history of religions" analysis more and more as the century progresses. [35]

The Struggle of the Literalists and Liberals Over Evolution

The nineteenth century was the great century of battle for the fundamentalists and the liberals. The orthodox tradition made one great attempt to suppress the growing contrapuntal tradition before the results of scientific study could win the hearts of the masses. The rise of Darwinism, the theory that man himself had evolved organically from the lower orders of creatures, was the last straw for the orthodox. Charles Darwin (1809–1882) published his epoch-making work, *On the Origin of Species*, in 1859. The whole first edition of 1,250 copies was sold out on the first day of issue. Darwin's ideas were not completely new, since they had been anticipated by Greek philosophers centuries before Christ, and had been written up by A. R. Wallace in 1858, a fact which forced Darwin to publicize his own findings.[36]

The orthodox considered Darwinism the theory of the devil, and they fought back, using every gap in Darwin's theory as an excuse to reject it. However, by the end of the nineteenth century, Darwinism was accepted as a valid theory, although with some modifications, by scholars everywhere. It is of interest to note that the battle of Genesis versus evolution was fought in England during the 1860's and 1870's, and thereafter quieted down with the victory of the liberals, but the struggle did not flare up in America until after World War I. The famous "Monkey Trial" in Tennessee did not take place until 1925, almost fifty years after the issue was settled in England.[37] What is almost fantastic in its indication of the intellectual lag between Europe and America is the fact that the anti-evolution law was not passed in Tennessee until March, 1925. That law stated that it was "unlawful for any teacher . . . to teach any theory that denies the story of the Divine Creation of man as taught in the Bible, and to teach instead that man has descended from a lower order of animals."[38] This case ended in the conviction of the teacher involved, John Scopes, but by its adverse publicity hastened the acceptance of the modern theory.

The most interesting and important elements in the Genesis versus evolution controversy were fought out in Europe in the nineteenth century. Little was added by the skirmishing in America in our century, except for the educational effects of that rather pathetic struggle on the younger generation. Perhaps the high point of the literalist-liberal debate was the quixotic attempt of Prime Minister Gladstone of England to demonstrate that the new scientific discoveries really supported the literalists' reading of the Old Testament.[39] Gladstone was answered by the famous Professor Huxley, who demolished all the orthodox arguments without difficulty. The general confluence of the results of the investigations of philologists, historians, geologists, classicists, archaeologists, and Bible scholars rushed into a mighty flood that washed away the shaky foundations of the orthodox tradition. After 1885, the orthodox churchmen either moved forward toward the liberal position or else reacted and became more and more fundamentalistic. Fundamentalism attempted (and still attempts) to deal with the modern learning by ignoring it. Meanwhile, the victorious liberals, in Germany, England, France, and America moved on to an even more sophisticated understanding of the Biblical text. One of the most important of the strands of this liberal study was the search for historical understanding of the "real" Jesus. In this "quest for the historical Jesus," liberalism, the modern expression of the contrapuntal tradition, suffered its first defeat.

The Quest for the Historical Jesus

Albert Schweitzer, surely one of the most attractive personalities in history and a prime example of the best in the contrapuntal tradition, dealt the theologians' quest for the real Jesus a death blow with the publication of *Von Reimarus zu Wrede: Eine Geschichte der Leben-Jesus-Forschung.*[40] Schweitzer, at the very beginning of the twentieth century (1906), sought to demonstrate that the scholars were on the wrong track in their studies of Jesus, and thus helped to direct the course of theological progress in our century. Schweitzer selected Reimarus and Wrede for his title, since Reimarus had been the first scholar to stress the importance of eschatology (belief in the events of the last days or the end of the age) to Jesus, and Wrede had sought to remove all reference to eschatology from Jesus' teaching. Schweitzer studied the many approaches to Jesus taken by scholars who ranged from pious to agnostic. He studied "Lives of Jesus" that made Jesus only another Jewish teacher and some lives that drew Jesus' portrait in lines taken from the nineteenth century. After them all, Schweitzer concluded that one can only understand Jesus as an eschatological prophet. Jesus came believing that he was to announce the arrival of the last days. Jesus preached an ethic for the brief interim between his work and the consummation of things. And, Schweitzer sadly concluded, since the last days did not arrive as Jesus predicted, Jesus was wrong. Jesus, in desperation, thought to force the advent of the Kingdom (the mark of the last days) by his witness in Jerusalem. Unfortunately, this ploy brought on Jesus' death. Thus, since we no longer are susceptible to eschatological preaching, Jesus cannot really be understood by us, and he remains as "One unknown." Schweitzer concluded that the quest for the historical Jesus had failed, for we can know little about the real Jesus, and what we do know we cannot understand. Thus the chief interest of liberal scholarship, and the chief content of "evangelical liberal" piety, evaporated under the heat of critical scholarship. The question of questions, whether a concrete event can be the center of a metaphysical reality (the Kingdom of God), remained, however. The question, put in another way, is this: Can the Jesus about whom we know so little be considered the center of history? Schweitzer's emphasis on eschatology revealed Jesus as a magnificent failure. Theologically this creates problems, although Jesus, insofar as we have knowledge of him, remains humanly admirable.

The decade that began with 1960 has seen a resurgence of interest in the historical Jesus, after a fifty-year lapse. Ernst Fuchs in Germany and several scholars in America, such as Norman Perrin and James M. Robinson, have revived the older liberal quest. But this time there is a difference, since all parties recognize that we can never know very much of the One who was a man for others so fully that he sacrificed himself. The " new quest " is but a part of our survey of the twentieth-century's religious situation, the part that still insists that Jesus is the greatest treasure in the Western tradition.

Chapter III
Radical Scholarship and Protestant Piety

THE BREAKDOWN of the rationalistic orthodox tradition was complete by the beginning of the twentieth century. The efforts of reactionary Christians to produce a platform, "The Five Fundamentals," [1] in America, which sparked the fundamentalist-modernist struggle in America was only the last-ditch stand of literalism, made possible only by the cultural lag between Europe and America. Theologians of competence in every Protestant communion had accepted the results of the great fund of scholarly findings and recognized that revelation does have a history and follows the kind of principles of internal development that are seen in the lives of cultures and sciences. The Word of God, after 1885, was generally recognized to be clothed in the words of men, and theologians paid great attention to the historical setting in which the elements of the Western Christian tradition had developed.

The Christian tradition now dominated by the new liberal theology was in no danger of being turned into a humanism, however. The scholars of Germany and England, and indeed the liberals of America, entrenched in the great university centers of Chicago, New York, and Boston, were, for the most part, deeply religious men. The first two decades of the present century were the heyday of the "Evangelical liberals" who sought manfully to make the gospel that Jesus preached available to modern men. Some of these pious representatives were members of distinctive schools of liberal theology, such as the Ritschlian and the Personalistic schools.[2]

The Ritschlian school of theology provides us with one of the clearest expressions of the influence of Kant on the modern religious outlook. Albrecht Benjamin Ritschl (1822–1889) was at first a disciple of Hegel, but he broke with this tradition in 1857 and struck out along Neo-Kantian lines. Briefly put, Neo-Kantianism rejected all natural theology and metaphysics, and stressed the role of the practical reason in our dealings with moral problems. This philosophy stressed the universality of the feeling of freedom and moral obligation among men, just as Kant had done. The philosophers Hermann Cohen (1842–1918) and Paul Natorp (1854–1924) became the leaders of this new movement.

Ritschl followed Neo-Kantianism in that he attempted to exclude metaphysics, and indeed the intellectual element, from Christianity. However, he went farther and sought to banish mysticism and emotion from the faith also. He severely criticized pietism in a famous work published in 1880, and rejected the starting point of Schleiermacher. Ritschl placed the will at the center of Christianity and developed the faith along moralistic lines. For Ritschl, religious beliefs are to be understood not as statements of fact but as value judgments (in German, *Werturteil*, a decision about the worth of something to an individual or group). Ritschl proceeded to interpret Christianity chiefly in terms of the Kingdom of God, which he considered to be the struggle of believers to organize mankind in accordance with the demands of Jesus for men to love one another. Love was Ritschl's chief religious category, God himself being defined only as love, or as " only Father." The " wrath of God " was de-emphasized, and God's loving acceptance of men in Christ was stressed.

However, the definition of Christianity produced by the various schools of the contrapuntal tradition, characterized as they were by their stress on love and man's sense of moral duty, were struck a heavy blow by the perverse destructiveness of European men in World War I. The shock of recognition that all was not right with "Christendom" that came from the spectacle of millions of deaths in 1914–1918 produced the reaction popularly known as the "crisis theology" or neo-orthodoxy of Karl Barth, Emil Brunner, Paul Tillich, and Rudolf Bultmann. We will postpone the discussion of this "Divorce of Mind and Spirit" in the Western tradition until Chapter IV. Now we turn to several outstanding figures who attempted to deal with the pre-World War I problems raised by the increasing feebleness of both the orthodox and the liberal versions of Christian theology. Some of these "great synthesizers" spanned the period of both World Wars, and will be dealt with at greater length in Chapter IV.

Wilhelm Herrmann: Piety Is Possible but Dogmatism Is Not

Wilhelm Herrmann (1846–1922) is one of those men whose greatest contribution to history was his charismatic quality as a teacher. Herrmann, little read in the second half of the twentieth century, continues to influence our religious outlook through his pupils Rudolf Bultmann and Karl Barth.

Herrmann was professor of dogmatic theology at the University of Marburg for many years, during which time he influenced several generations of theologians. Herrmann wrote little; his *Systematic Theology* [3] is a book of less than one hundred pages. His most influential work is the classic *The Communion of the Christian with God*,[4] published in 1886. Theology, for Herrmann, is the description of religion as a historical reality perceived by those who experience it. Religion means seeing the working of God in the events of life. Herrmann declared: "We possess [religion] only when we come to the consciousness that God is working upon us in some particular situation as the power which saves us." [5] Like Ritschl, to whose school he belonged, Herrmann understood Christian doctrines in the light of value judgments. Christ is valued by

Christians as being what only God can be, and therefore God is Jesus. Christ opened men's eyes to the goodness of God, so the "historical Jesus" is important for Herrmann's thought. However, Herrmann was well aware of the impossibility of securing an objective picture of the historical Jesus, so he moved to what he called "the inner life of Jesus" (his communion with God) for the basis of his system.

For Herrmann, "our own communion with God" is the most important, most fundamental, theme in religion. He believed that the theological battles of the nineteenth century had come about because men had lost sight of this fact. On the other hand, Herrmann felt impelled to write of Luther's conception of Christian communion because "modern pietism and liberal churchmanship" espoused an ideal of piety that grew up in Roman Catholicism rather than out of the Reformation. Thus the book was keenly polemical, and necessitated a second edition with eighty extra pages six years later (1892), removing some barbs and explaining others. For Herrmann, Jesus is a living figure whose inner life is open to us through a pious reading of the Scriptures as well as through communing with him here and now, through faith. Thus, the reality of God, which cannot be established by natural theology or metaphysics, is established in Herrmann's view on the ground of the communion we have with God through Christ. But the question that must still be faced is whether the inner life of Jesus is any more exempt from the probabilities of historical scholarship than are the other elements that make up the so-called historical Jesus.

Albert Schweitzer: Christ Mysticism Not the Historical Jesus the Basis of Christian Faith

As we noted above, Schweitzer brought the quest for the historical Jesus to an end for a period of fifty years (1906–1956), by demonstrating that no one could ever establish just what the historical Jesus was like. Schweitzer wrote:

But the truth is it is not Jesus as historically known, but Jesus as spiritually arisen within men, who is significant for our time and can help it. Not the historical Jesus, but the spirit which goes forth from Him and in the spirits of men strives for new influence and rule, is that which overcomes the world.[6]

Schweitzer sought to put in the place of the historical Jesus the theological outlook he found in his study of Paul, which Schweitzer, along with Adolf Deissmann,[7] called Christ-mysticism. Schweitzer once wrote that Paul's words in Rom., ch. 8, that "he who has not the Spirit of Christ is not his" have made a deep impression upon him. He declared that it is far more important to have the Spirit of Jesus than anything else in Christianity.[8] Schweitzer found a true description of possession of the Spirit of Christ in Paul. Schweitzer, who profoundly believed that Jesus taught a message of eschatological fulfillment which proved to be erroneous, believed that we must renounce our efforts to recapture the faith of the man Jesus and seek instead a surrender to God as Paul conceived it, as a union with the Spirit of love and self-sacrifice which was manifested in Jesus Christ. We must not attempt to believe what Jesus believed so much as we must believe as Paul believed and live as Jesus lived. Living like Jesus, for Schweitzer, means having a feeling of unity with God who is Being as such and practicing a reverence for all of life. Schweitzer made an extensive study of mysticism: primitive, which ushers in magical beliefs, and intellectual, which reflects upon the relation of the individual to the universality of being itself. Schweitzer also studied the German mystical tradition and Indian mysticism. He felt that the mysticism of Paul was different and greater than any of these. Paul's mysticism was not primitive, nor was it intellectual, for it did not seek unity with God as the Ultimate Ground of Being. Paul never speaks of being one with God but of being one with Christ and through union with Christ being related to God as a son. Thus Paul has no God-mysticism, only a Christ-mysti-

cism by means of which man comes into relation with God.[9]
Schweitzer concludes that Christianity rightly understood is
a Christ-mysticism in the Pauline manner. However, Schweitzer taught that Christ-mysticism must be joined to ethics,
especially the ethics of reverence for life. Schweitzer taught
that mysticism does not exist for its own sake, but like the stalk
of a flower, it exists to produce the blossom of ethics.

Schweitzer attempted to meet the demands of the modern
age for a gospel shorn of myth and pointed toward the problems of actual life by conclusively demonstrating that the
original setting of the gospel was not tenable for modern
presentation. He frankly admitted that religious truth varies
from age to age, but he thought we could find in the teaching
of Jesus a religion of love which was as viable in the twentieth century as it was in the first. Without doubt Schweitzer
made a noble attempt and has been himself the best argument for his vision of what the gospel is, but the increasing
note of criticism directed toward him in the last decade of his
life already reveals the large element of moralism and European paternalism that was included in his concept of
reverence for life.[10] It is not clear that Schweitzer has discovered the key to a true viability for Christianity in our
times, because reverence for life and for the human Jesus is
too apt to pass into lofty humanism instead of remaining in
some way distinctively the expression of the Western Christian tradition. If Schweitzer's answers are generally accepted,
we may indeed see the arising of what Dietrich Bonhoeffer
called religionless Christianity. Many of us would be happier
with that turn of affairs, but it would not satisfy the bulk of
those people who call themselves Christians.

Rudolf Bultmann: Making the Gospel Intelligible to Our Time

Rudolf Bultmann [11] was born in 1884, in Oldenberg, Germany. In 1966 he was living in retirement, a retirement often

broken by visits from theologians and his former pupils at Marburg University. Men from all over the world, not only his "Old Marburgers," go to visit Bultmann to listen to his temperate bluntness concerning modern theological problems. There is good reason for these visits, for the often denounced Bultmann is one of the three or four most creative and decisive theologians of the twentieth century. His work, in earlier years done by the form-critical method (*Formgeschichte*), and in his later years by the method of demythologizing, has affected the development of theology not only in Protestantism but in Roman Catholicism and Judaism as well. It is a truism that the majority of educated and interested religious people have heard of demythologizing, but that few understand what it means.

Bultmann represents the side of systematic theology that might be called the *synthetic camp*, which, in opposition to the analytical camp of Karl Barth, insists that we must approach the Bible from where we are as modern men. It will be recognized immediately that this synthetic analytical approach is the position of this book, which recognizes the necessity of man's understanding of the world view that characterizes his innermost thought. The analytical camp, on the other hand, claims that the Bible may and must be understood from within the world view presented in the Bible itself.

Its exponents insist that by analyzing the Bible texts in the light of one another we discover a completely self-contained, self-sufficient, and God-revealed world view from within which we may deduce all the necessary procedural principles for correctly interpreting the texts, and hence for determining valid doctrine. The dogmatic endeavor in effect is a mental auger boring and spiraling ever deeper into the Scriptural material.[12]

One cannot help admiring the intellectual fortitude of Barth and those few theologians like Hendrik Kraemer [13] who follow Barth's "philosophy" of Biblical interpretation,[14] but one also cannot help feeling that they do not recognize the practical necessity of preaching to people where they are in language that they can understand. It is interesting to note that the analytical school includes among its followers a great portion of the Protestant clergy, but it is Bultmann and Tillich, the chief spokesmen for the synthetic school, who have been most concerned with the problems of preaching. Bultmann's whole effort to demythologize the gospel can be seen as a grand attempt at synthesis of the modern mind and the Christian spirit. Even the highly intellectual Tillich devoted a good deal of his effort to preaching to college and university audiences, attempting to make the faith intelligible to the younger generation.

Rudolf Bultmann [15] belongs to that little group of religious men who were profoundly affected by the tragedy of World War I. Like Paul Tillich, who felt his whole world view change as he looked upon the carnage of the terrible Battle of Champagne in World War I, Bultmann served as a chaplain in the German Army. Bultmann has written of the awful misery of the Western front and of the difficulty of preaching to men who had experienced the utter breakdown of the Christian civilization of Europe. More than church steeples were knocked down by the heavy guns of the contending forces — the belief in progress, the belief in the superiority of reason over unreason, and, indeed, the belief in the goodness of God as taught by the church dissolved with the normal landscape of the countryside under the battering of the gunfire. Bultmann reports that anxious soldiers who heard his sermons behind the trenches asked: "What do you mean by resurrection, Padre? Do you mean that dead men's bones rise up? You can't mean that, can you, Padre?"

In the words of a later German theologian, Dietrich Bonhoeffer, "the world had come of age," and it was high time for someone to come up with intelligible answers to the problems of modern men. This is what the preacher, Rudolf Bultmann, set out to do — for Bultmann is essentially a preacher, a proclaimer of the Word of God — and it is this interest in proclamation that motivates the scholarly labor that has filled his life.

The key to preaching, according to Bultmann, is the principle of interpretation, known as hermeneutic. Bultmann's work, therefore, is essentially involved with hermeneutic, with the problems and the practice of the interpretation of the Bible in order to proclaim its message. Essentially, the tack taken by Bultmann is a stress on history. He searches for the essence of Christianity, and seeks it in the doctrines of the church that have developed historically. Bultmann says of Christianity: " The first thing [in it] is a new sense of history and the historically significant existence of man."

Bultmann says that the decisive thing in Christianity is that man is now no longer pointed toward the past but toward the future. World history for the Christian, as for the Hebrew prophets, is a meaningful whole which takes place over against that God who is related to history in a purposeful way. Of course, Bultmann knows that to think of God in a relationship to history is to engage in " mythological " thought. Whenever we speak of the two great opposites, the divine and the world, in terms of correlation, we are engaged in mythical thinking.

For many centuries simple Christians believed in the literal accuracy of the reports contained in the Bible.[16] They accepted, apparently without too great a strain on their reasoning ability, the literalness of the belief in the three-storied structure of the universe reflected in the New Testament, with the earth presented as the center of the universe, with hell beneath, and with heaven above. The earth itself was thought of in terms of supernatural activity, with God and the angels arrayed on the side of the saints in their unending struggle with Satan. Man was not thought to be in control of his own life, but rather, evil spirits might take control of a man at any time, or God might, conversely, inspire his thoughts and guide man to fulfill heaven's purposes. History was indeed conceived of as a grand tapestry of "holy history" in which the God who created the world in six days and rested on the seventh day pursued his inscrutable will in man or by man, regardless of a man's personal choice.

But after the Renaissance and the rise of the *Aufklärung*, it became increasingly difficult for educated men to accept the Bible's mythological world view. Men had rounded the earth and knew its dimensions quite well. They were learning what they called "natural laws," and they were committed to causality. Whatever happened, happened because of some prior cause, and so on ad infinitum. The elements of the world, including man, behaved in regular and "lawful" ways. Thus the days of an unquestioned acceptance of the mythological world view of the Bible were numbered after about 1700. Of course, among certain groups of Christians, such as the lesser-educated Roman Catholics and the Protestants who would in time be known as pietists and (later) "fundamentalists," a rough-and-ready acceptance of the myth of the Scriptures would continue right down to our own day. But even these groups contain many a believer who, in Markus Barth's phrase, "pays his tribute to demythologizing by doing it himself." At any rate, today there is no longer any doubt among theologians as to the mythological world view expressed by the New Testatment (and the Old Testament), and that the reports of the Synoptic Gospels (as well as John and Paul) are couched in symbols and myths.

Bultmann tells us that "the real purpose of myth is not to present an objective picture of the world as it is, but to express man's understanding of himself in the world in which he lives. Myth should be interpreted not cosmologically, but anthropologically, or better still, existentially." The myth speaks of the "other world" (of the divine) in terms of this world, and of the gods in terms derived from human life. It is an expression of man's conviction that the origin and the purpose of the world in which man lives are to be sought not within the world but beyond it. Myth expresses man's awareness, then, that he is not the lord of his own being.

Bultmann tried to distinguish between the true scandalon (offense) of the cross — the act of God in Jesus for our salvation — and the pseudo scandala or offenses which lie in the stories about a virgin birth, etc. The purpose of demythologization is not to make religion more acceptable to modern man by trimming the traditional Biblical texts but to make clearer to modern man what the Christian faith is. He must be confronted with the issue of decision, be provoked to decision by the fact that the stumbling block to faith, the scandalon, is peculiarly disturbing to man in general, not only to modern man.

Therefore, his attempt begins by clearing away the false stumbling blocks created for modern man by the fact that his world view is dominated by science. As such, the real problem is the hermeneutic one. This involves grasping adequately the meaning of the text which is to be interpreted; and it involves the conveying of that meaning intelligibly to those who are asking for the interpretation.

Bultmann contends that the truth of the Christian gospel is independent of any world view, either past, present, or future. He says the New Testament kerygma's (i.e., proclamation's) world view is mythological and is therefore unacceptable to modern man whose thinking has been shaped by science and is no longer mythological. Therefore, modern man should not be expected to accept the mythological view of the New Testament, for there is nothing specifically Christian in this mythical view of the world as such. It is simply a cosmology of a prescientific age. In fact, it is impossible to do so because no one can adopt a view of the world by his own volition. It is already determined for him by his place in history.

Therefore, if the truth of the New Testament proclamation

is to be preserved, the only way is to demythologize it. We cannot save the kerygma by selecting some of its features and subtracting others and thus reduce the amount of mythology in it. In this program our motive must not be to make the New Testament relevant to the modern world at all costs; but rather, the question is whether the New Testament message consists exclusively of mythology or whether it actually demands the elimination of myth if it is to be understood as it is meant to be.

The real purpose of myth is not to present an objective picture of the world as it is, but to express man's understanding of himself in the world in which he lives. Myth speaks of the power or powers which man supposes he experiences as the ground and limit of his world and of his own activity and suffering. Man describes these powers in terms derived from the visible world, with its tangible objects and forms, and from human life, with its feelings, motives, and potentialities. Myth is an expression of man's awareness that he is not lord of his own being, his sense of dependence on those forces which hold sway beyond the confines of the known. Myth expresses man's belief that in this state of dependence he can be delivered from the forces within the visible world.

Bultmann's attempt to make Christianity understandable to modern men beyond the point of simply retelling the literal stories of the Gospels comes from his belief that in Christianity man does find the grace of God. This grace he interprets in terms borrowed from existentialist philosophy, particularly that of Heidegger. He tells us that the salvation which we receive from our own confrontation with the crucified Christ proclaimed in the Gospels is freedom from ourselves. We like to think that we are free, but we are not, for we are bound to the decisions made in our own past. Our human freedom is only relative freedom, but the freedom that comes from seeing that our own plans and hopes for the future, our anxiousness for tomorrow, are really senseless, for we must ultimately fail in that we must die. But in looking at Christ and seeing his sacrifice as being greater than human success in that in his failure he was made free to love, we are radically freed from ourselves, from the past, and from the future. We can receive this freedom only as a gift, only in the decision which takes Jesus Christ as the decisive event of history in which God puts to an end the old world of human striving and gives man a new opportunity to live free for others, free for love. Such a man is "a new man in Christ." Thus Bultmann proclaims the "paradox of Christ" who is at once the Jesus of history, who is part of the past, and at the same time the ever-present Lord who lives in the preaching of the church.[17]

Bultmann has made himself liable to the fear and dislike of a great many Christians, both theologians and laymen, because of his boldness in diagnosing the problem of theology as being the problem of demythologizing the gospel. Naturally, every person with a tendency toward conservatism has reacted against Bultmann's platform. However, Bultmann has also made himself liable to the criticism of fellow liberal theologians who share his belief — which is, beyond question, a correct belief — that the gospel is cast in mythological form. The basic critique made of Bultmann is that the modern scientific viewpoint by which he proposes to judge the mythology of the gospel is itself not a truly scientific platform. It is often charged, by theologians and philosophers, that Bultmann's modern world view is really that of the older physics of Descartes. Bultmann certainly does seem to speak of science as the recognition of natural laws that result in a philosophy of mechanistic determinism. Jacques Maritain[18] has attacked Bultmann on this point with some degree of truth. Undoubtedly, Bultmann does not take into account the tentativeness of modern physics, such as the recognition of Heisenberg's uncertainty principle which has resulted in a revolution in the world view of modern science.[19]

A further problem that Bultmann's emphasis upon man's historical self-understanding brings to the fore is the problem which Kant saw long ago, the fact that man's existence and man's understanding of the world both implies and does not imply the existence of God. Thus Bultmann's platform produces a new antinomy. It is enlightening to see that some of Bultmann's followers, such as the theologian Fritz Buri, have suggested that the message of Christianity needs to be recast in the thought forms of existential philosophy and not just translated from mythological forms to modern forms. There are indications that some thinkers believe that it is quite possible to accept what Bultmann has to say about the freedom that comes to the individual without putting any particular stress upon Christ. Shubert Ogden and other thinkers who derive part of their thought from the process philosophy of Whitehead have implied that the authentic existence which Bultmann defines as salvation in the world at large is possible apart from the historical Christ. It seems possible that Bultmann's position could be accepted without any belief in God at all. Thus to a degree, Bultmann's program of demythologization has contributed to our present situation where many are saying that God is dead.

Paul Tillich: Making the Gospel Intelligible Through a Process of Deliteralization

Paul Tillich [20] (1886–1965) was perhaps the best-known Protestant theologian of our time. Indeed, we might well remove the qualification "Protestant" and say he was the best-known theologian of our time. Thousands of people who have no connection with the church read his works, especially people on university campuses who are apt to ponder his published sermons as well as his more popular works of philosophical theology. In many respects he almost single-handedly reversed the once scornful attitude of intellectuals toward the church and made "theologizing" an honored and respected activity at the chief seats of American learning. Harvard University selected Tillich to be a "University Professor" and made him a member of the Institute for Advanced Study, which pursues intellectual research on the frontiers of knowledge. All of this achievement seems the more amazing when we consider that Tillich began a "second career" in America at the age of forty-seven, after first establishing himself as a leading theologian in Germany.

Paul Johannes Tillich was born in Brandenburg, in eastern Germany. His father was a Lutheran superintendent and a successful clergyman. In 1911 he received his Ph.D. degree and in 1912 he completed his theological studies and was ordained a Lutheran pastor. The year 1914 saw the outbreak of World War I, and young Tillich joined the Imperial German Army as a war chaplain. This great and bloody struggle which changed the face of Europe was the end of Tillich's preparation for philosophy and was the beginning of personal reflections that would lead him in later years to attempt to answer the questions and needs of the modern world of revolution and crisis with the eternal answers of the Christian message. In four terrible years, 1914–1918, Tillich witnessed the horrors of modern warfare in the senseless bloodletting in the trenches on the Western front. Imperial Germany was defeated by the Allies, and the old order in Germany collapsed. Revolution and bankruptcy faced that great nation. Tillich desired to help his country recover itself and build a new, more healthy social order, and to this end embraced "religious socialism." "Religious socialism" meant for Tillich the application of the prophetic demands for justice for all men to the serious social problems of defeated and demoralized Germany.

By socialism, Tillich never meant Marxism in the sense of Russian Communism. What Tillich did adopt was the "democratic Marxism" of the German Socialist movement, which called for the breakdown of the now corrupt remnants of the old Prussian aristocracy and the building of a modern nation based on the universal right to vote, freedom for workers to

combine in labor unions, and a society based on equal opportunity for all. The religious socialists actually called for a society much like that which we have built in the United States.

The experiment of the Weimar Republic failed in the post-
World War I Germany and Adolf Hitler's " national socialism "
came to power in 1933. One of Hitler's first moves was to dis-
miss Tillich from his professorship at the University of Frank-
furt. Thus in 1933, Tillich accepted an invitation to come to
Union Theological Seminary in New York City. The leading
American theologian Reinhold Niebuhr [21] had brought about
Tillich's invitation to the United States, for he shared much of
the concerns of the European religious socialists and also ad-
mired Tillich's published works.

Most of Tillich's work, up to 1933, was concerned with what
he called a " theology of culture." He saw theology as a mediation, a mediation of the eternal truth of the gospel about Jesus
the Christ and the changing experiences of individuals and
groups living in history.

Tillich's goal was to show that theology has two poles: one
pole, the eternal message of Christ; the other pole, the " existential " (i.e., life) situation. Theology must be truly theology,
that is, the mystery of God (*theos*) made understandable
(*logos*) to men where they live in history. The technical name
for this kind of theologizing is " dialectical theology." Much of
this emphasis can be seen in his book *The Religious Situation*.[22]

Tillich has made a place for himself, and for the eternal
message of the gospel in an age of doubt, anxiety, and despair
in the intellectual world of America. At first, few people outside of Union Seminary had heard of Tillich; little of his work
was written in English. But by hard work he mastered the new
tongue and within a few years produced all his work in English. It is amusing to think that the great theologian's works
were once translated from German into English, but now the
later works have to be translated from English into German.
Tillich spent twenty years teaching at Union Seminary. His

love for the Seminary can be seen in his statement: "If New York is the bridge between continents, Union Seminary is the lane of that bridge on which the churches of the world move." [23]

After retirement from Union Seminary, Dr. Tillich became University Professor at Harvard for a number of years and then accepted the position of John P. Nuveen Distinguished Professor of Theology at the Divinity School of the University of Chicago, a position he held to the end of his life. [24]

Tillich is one of our century's great synthesizers in that the aim of his work has been to make it possible for modern men to hold fast to the insights and grace available to them in the Christian tradition. [25] Tillich has been criticized for the radicality of his presentation of Christianity, and named by some of the most radical thinkers of our time as one of the " fathers " of the " God is dead " theology, a charge he always refuted. We will briefly describe Tillich's theological method and then analyze his treatment of the doctrine of God in order to assess correctly Tillich's place in the present breakup of the Western Christian tradition.

The theology of Paul Tillich is a philosophical or ontological theology in which every doctrine, symbol, and concept is traced back to one of the structures of being itself. Yet, with this metaphysical foundation and structure, the Bible remains the primary source of revelation for Tillich. Where Luther, Barth, and Brunner have spurned the aid of philosophy in the systematic task, Tillich has welcomed and made use of the entire history of philosophical thought in his theological writings. Thus, in addition to the Bible, Tillich sees church history, the history of Christian theology, and that great fund of the world's wisdom found in other religions, and in art, as a general revelation. This is the chief distinguishing characteristic of Tillich's theology from that of most Protestant theologians. However, the differences can be stressed too harshly, for Tillich's theology is kerygmatic, i.e., a proclaiming of the good news, as well as apologetic, or explanatory in its nature. He sees the sources for theology in the history of Christian thought and in general revelation as useful sources only insofar as they are similar to the content of the original document which contains the record of the events on which Christianity is based, the Bible itself.[26]

Tillich is an apologetic theologian in that he sees his task as one of making the Christian message intelligible to and acceptable to modern men.[27] He sees the human predicament as one in which men are hindered from receiving help from the eternal message of Christ by the obscure cast of many theologies and by the mythological form of most preaching. His desire is to interpret the great symbols of Christianity in terms of modern existentialist philosophy, so as to make the power of Christ's message available to men today. The method by which Tillich does this is that of correlation, which means that Tillich gives the answers of Christian faith to the questions asked by modern men.[28] Basically this correlative method is predicated on the need to harmonize the existence of two similar but different approaches to the discovery and elucidation of the situation and prospects of mankind, those of philosophy and theology.

Tillich begins his system by declaring that we can approach the understanding of Christian faith only in an existential manner, i.e., with our present life situation in mind. God does not give answers to questions that men have not asked. Thus we must start where we are in our life situation and pose the problems that we face in this existence as questions, and only then turn to the revelation of God for the answers. In this task, philosophy poses the questions and theology supplies the answers on the basis of the three sources of theological insight mentioned above. Tillich defines this method of correlation in the following way: " Philosophy is defined as that cognitive endeavor in which the question of being is asked on the basis of an analysis of the human situation, thus revealing the

brokenness, ambiguities and problems of human existence." [29]
Theology is based on revelation or the experience of men who
have gained insights into the depths of the structures of being
(which reveals itself to man).[30] Thus, those who have had
such revelatory experiences have been transformed in the
center of their being by becoming aware of being's wholeness
in the ecstatic depths of human reason. Such experiences sup-
ply the answers to the questions posed by philosophy. Therefore, Tillich starts with incompleteness, brokenness, and despair in the existentialist sense, and ends with completeness,
wholeness, and a kind of "union with God" in the sense of
classical Christian theology.[31] In order to have this correlation,
there must be a point of contact, and this contact is the structure of being itself. For Tillich, man, nature, and God are
joined together in the structure of being; indeed, God is the
structure of being, the Ground of Being, although not being
determined by that structure.[32]

Tillich clearly states that everything we say about God is
symbolic except the statement that everything we say about
God is symbolic. However, the phrase "God is Being Itself"
may be considered literal; although even in such an abstrac-
tion there is a mixture of the symbolic (ecstatic) and the nonsymbolic (literal). This is true because these terms form the
boundary line at which the symbolic and nonsymbolic modes
of speech converge.[33] In all events, God is the inexhaustible
depth within the structure of being in which man and nature
participate. But man has distorted the basic structures of being by his sin, for becoming actual (existential) means becoming somehow separated from the Divine Ground and becoming
distorted and alienated. Thus there appears a "gap" between
essence (the Ground) and existence (man's actuality). This
gap, called finitude, alienation, brokenness, or sin, is overcome
– and God and man are brought together – in Jesus as the
Christ, the Bearer of the New Being, which is nothing else than
unity with the Divine Ground, i.e., a reestablishment of the

continuity between God and man by an "overcoming" of
the discontinuities between them. In Jesus as the bearer of the
New Reality the structure of being is essentially exemplified
even amid the existential distortions of it ("under the conditions of existence") in human history. Thus Jesus is man as he
is "meant to be;" he is man "transparent" to the depths of
being itself. Here is that unity with God for which all men
(consciously or unconsciously) yearn, for as Augustine has
said: "Thou hast made us [men] for thyself, and our hearts are
restless, till they rest in thee." [34]

The structure of Tillich's ontological theology hinges on
his vision of the eternal tension between being and nonbeing.
Tillich's concern for establishing an ontological foundation for
his system (and for the Christian faith) is very clear in his
refusal to rest at any point until he has laid bare the ultimate
structures of reality, i.e., being, nonbeing, existence, and essence. Then, in each instance, Tillich seeks to relate the problems of the human predicament (as revealed by an existential analysis) to their ontological referent. He develops the
"answers" of revelation to the "question" raised by his existential analysis on this basis. Man exists preeminently among
all creatures because he is aware of his existence and of the
possibility of his own death, i.e., his own nonbeing. Man, as
was know him, exists in anxiety, not fear, for fear has an object and is psychological, but man suffers from *Angst*, which
is ontological anxiety and has no objective referent but arises
out of our awareness of our possible nonbeing. This is "the
ontological shock" in which we become aware that there
might be nothing rather than something. Everything in Tillich's system works out from this point.

God, according to Tillich, is the Ground of Being. In the
symbolic language that we are forced to use when speaking of
God, God is the creator of the universe. In God alone is full-
ness of being. For in him all the ontological elements are perfectly balanced, whereas they are polarized, i.e., divided along

the subject-object continuum in man and nature. These ontological elements are the polarities of: (1) individualization
and participation; (2) dynamics and form; (3) freedom and
destiny.

Our lives as men are lived under these polarities, of which
the most basic expression is that of the split between subject
and object into I-Thou or I-it, which Tillich calls the basic
ontological polarity of self and world.[35]

In the universe there are also categories that express the
ontological situation. They are time, space, causality, and substance. In God all these elements and categories are perfectly
in balance, but not so in the universe, where man lives in a
condition which is not one of being or of nonbeing, but is a
mixture of being and nonbeing that is called finitude or existence.

Tillich's theology, although it was designed to enable man
to be both a member of the modern intellectual community
and a Christian, is not altogether successful. There are several
reasons for this, some of which are in no wise faults. Tillich's
failure, if we can speak of failure this soon after the appearance of his major works (1951–1963), is the inbred resistance
of modern men to the kind of philosophical thinking that
Tillich represents. While Tillich is known as an existentialist,
a serious study of his works reveals that he is actually in the
tradition of German idealism and believes that there is a reality behind the words he uses, such as "being" and "spirit."
For Tillich, there is a unity of thought and being just as there
was for Hegel and nineteenth-century idealists. This kind of
thinking is not understood by many people today. In his "In-
terrogation" in the volume *Philosophical Interrogations*,[36]
Tillich makes clear that there are essences in his belief behind
the words used in his philosophy. He declares in that place
that Americans are "nominalists by birth" and recognizes
that this kind of outlook makes it difficult for modern Americans to understand and accept the Christian faith. This factor

in our modern life cannot be blamed on Tillich, but we must admit that it undercuts much of what Tillich has tried to do.

The reason why radical thinkers, such as Altizer, have claimed Tillich as a source of the modern radical theology is Tillich's lifelong struggle against the crudities of orthodox theism. Tillich, however, is well within the main stream of philosophical theology in his insistence that we cannot elevate a portion of the finite to the status of God without falling into idolatry. In *The Courage to Be*,[37] Tillich spoke of "theism transcended," pointing out the inevitable idolatry that occurs whenever men speak of God as personal or connect God with some portion of the universe. In *Biblical Religion and the Search for Ultimate Reality*,[38] Tillich points out that our encounter with the God we designate as personal includes the encounter with the God who is the ground of everything personal and as such is not a person. Tillich's reasoning is spelled out in his famous essay "Two Types of Philosophy of Religion." [39] Tillich actually is arguing for what we may call correctly the majesty of God, but the ordinary layman who does not understand theological terms and the so-called orthodox theologian who does understand and should know better than to attack Tillich at this point both surmise that Tillich is denying that there *is* a God. Thus, an unfortunate result of Tillich's attempt to teach the Christian doctrine of God accurately has been the widespread impression that he did not "believe in" God. Nothing could be farther from the truth; yet the insistence of the self-appointed orthodox theologians who continue to speak of God as personal without qualifying explanation, and their desire to attack anyone who uses language different from their own, has given the impression that Tillich was an atheist. This is doubly unfortunate because Tillich genuinely sought to be faithful to the message of the Bible and to the historical self-understanding of mankind in our time. It is to be hoped that, although Tillich did not leave a school of theology behind him, the undoubted widespread influence he has had on younger theologians and younger intellectuals of all disciplines will continue to deepen and expand. As difficult as the construction of a workable method of correlation is, it is the only method that ultimately enables the theologian to speak to man where he is. Thus, Tillich's attempt is a move in the right direction (although it is not now successful) and points beyond itself to a restoration of an intelligent, appreciative awareness of the eternal message of a Christianity.[40]

The great synthesizers, Herrmann, Schweitzer, Bultmann, and Tillich, have had their day. At the time this chapter was written, only Bultmann was still living (at age eighty-one). The valiant attempts to replace the framework of the Christian faith which was washed away, because it deserved to be washed away, by the rise of modern scholarship with a piety based on the "inner life of Jesus," or with "Christ-mysticism," or with "authentic existence," or even with "the New Being" fragmentarily experienced under the conditions of existence, all failed, at least for our decade. The rise of the radical theology with its declaration that God is dead demonstrates the failure either of the synthetic theologians or of the church which did not fully accept their great syntheses. It is the contention of this book that much of what Schweitzer, Bultmann, and Tillich did was not a failure, but that the failure lies in the idolatry and ignorance of the Christian church's leaders and theologians. The elements for the reconstruction of Christianity in the twentieth century have been offered to the church and they have been spurned. But either way, the result is that the church and its theology have failed and we have entered the era of "the death of God." [41]

Chapter IV
The Divorce of Mind and Spirit

DESPITE THE EFFORTS of the great synthesizers, those theological thinkers who have made heroic attempts to preserve the Catholic substance of our Christian heritage while accepting (as we all must) our modern historical self-understanding, the past decade has witnessed the frank admission (by some radically honest thinkers) that the mental and spiritual life of man has experienced a great divorce. Our epoch, the era of the awareness of the "death of God," has experienced the final breakup of the unity of mind and spirit so long artificially preserved by rationalistic orthodoxy. The final result of the Kantian critical philosophy (the foundation of modern thought) has been the awareness that man can have no knowledge of God, and hence we must either accept Barth's revelation-based theology (which entails the sacrifice of our intellect) or confess with Tillich that all statements about God are symbolic. If these two options are discarded, we can only declare that God is dead. In this chapter we shall investigate some of the external and internal influences that have brought us to this crisis in our religious lives. We shall find that all the elements we identify drive irresistibly toward a radical reexamination of the Christian doctrine of God.

External Influences That Contributed to the Divorce of Mind and Spirit

Neither the orthodox Western tradition nor the contrapuntal tradition were quite the same after Kant's far-reaching critique of the pure and practical reason. Man's mind was seen as a disciplined area in which the noumena and phenomena, the internal structures of the mind itself and the sense impressions that furnished the mind's content, were brought together in an analytic way. In this arena, there was no place for the synthetic ideas of self, God, and world. Only by an act of self-transcendence, by passing beyond the "given," could the mind project the transcendental ideal of the pure reason, which is the aim, goal, and limit of all thought, God.

But these ideas were functional in the European mentality for one hundred and twenty-five years without producing the reactions we have witnessed in our lifetime. What made the difference? The difference is the breakdown of the framework of Western Christian culture that held the mind and spirit (the transcendent) together during the first one hundred and twenty-five years of the critical philosophy. A series of external crises and movements destroyed the setting of the Christian doctrine of God. The first of these crises was World War I. History may prove that the last casualty of that terrible conflict was not removed from the "Missing in Action" to the "Killed in Action" list for forty years, for that casualty was the orthodox doctrine of God.

The Earthquake That Weakened the Fabric of Western European Culture: 1914–1918

In Chapter III, we discussed the effects of World War I upon Rudolf Bultmann and Paul Tillich. In a very real sense, the theological methods elected by these outstanding leaders of the synthetic, liberal tradition were dictated by their experiences at the front.

The brutalities of modern warfare were indeed enough to shake the optimism of the liberal humanism that circulated in Europe and America prior to 1914. The exposure of young idealistic thinkers such as the German theological students, Bultmann and Tillich, and the budding poets of England, Wilfred Owen (1893–1918), Siegfried Sassoon (1886–   ), and Rupert Brooke (1887–1915), to the insanity of mass death could be expected to produce crises of faith in them. However, if the inner arrangement of Western Christianity had not yet been disarrayed by the internal struggle between orthodox and liberal, we would not expect the whole fabric of Western mankind's faith to have weakened as it demonstrably did after World War I. It is worth noting that neither the sensitive Germans nor the sensitive Englishmen became atheists because of their experiences, although each of them came to the same insight which Tillich expressed in 1914, that his entire world view was dead. The poems left by Owen, Sassoon, and Brooke speak not so much of the failure of God, but of the failure of man and of the failure of the church.

A close reading of the British war poets reveals no hatred of God, but a hatred of what mankind has done in his civilization in the name of God. Wilfred Owen has written of this perversion in his famous "Arms and the Boy": "And God will grow no talons at his heels." [1]

In a different way, but in response to the same kind of feelings, Bultmann and Tillich reacted against the orthodox theology and the middle-class culture that it supported. The crisis of Western European culture was brought on by the sudden experience of insight among the intellectuals that the whole framework of Western culture was mendacious, a lie that supported the ruling classes and the religion held so inviolate by the orthodox, and was but a prop for the *status quo*. As long as this framework of culture had contributed to human progress, to world peace, and to the advancement of science in constructive ways, it made it possible for those in power to remain in power and — what is to the point here — it made it possible for men to hold to an unspecified theism that took God's goodness and his very existence for granted. Christianity, the religious genius of Europe for fifteen hundred years, had imposed this general religiosity upon the art, politics, social order, and economics of Europe. Now, when that cultural framework broke apart, the God that had been placed at the apex of European culture fell because there was nothing left to support belief in him. As long as the framework held together, it was natural for all parties, politicians and scientists, writers and theologians, to speak of God in a general way. The liberals of the eighteenth and nineteenth centuries had reacted against this idea of God as a piece of cultural furniture and, on the intellectual level, had destroyed the rationalizations that had supported this concept of God. The full impact of what Kant, Schleiermacher, Ritschl, and others had done did not become readily apparent until the external props of the nineteenth-century humanitarian culture failed. World War I destroyed the skeleton of orthodox Christianity, for only the skeleton was left. The internal organs had been eaten away long before by the advance of scholarly thought.

The popular novelist, Erich Maria Remarque, in his novel *All Quiet on the Western Front* writes of this process:

We were still crammed full of vague ideas which gave to life, and to the war also, an ideal and almost romantic character. We were trained in the army for ten weeks and in this time learned that a bright button is weightier than four volumes of Schopenhauer. At first astonished, then embittered, and finally indifferent, we recognized that what matters is not the mind but the boot brush, not intelligence but the system, not freedom but drill. We became soldiers with eagerness and enthusiasm, but they have done everything to knock that out of us. After three weeks it was no longer incomprehensible to us that a braided postman should have more authority over us than had formerly our parents, our teachers, and the whole gamut of culture from Plato to Goethe. With our young, awakened eyes

we saw that the classical conception of the Fatherland held
by our teachers resolved itself here into a renunciation of
personality such as one would not ask of the meanest servant —
salutes, springing to attention, parade-marches . . .[2]

At the very end of his book, Remarque speaks of the terrible
effect of war experiences upon his generation. His concluding
chapter is almost a prophecy of what was to come after 1918:

Had we returned home in 1916, out of the suffering and the
strength of our experiences we might have unleashed a storm.
Now if we go back we will be weary, broken, burnt out,
rootless, and without hope. We will not be able to find our way
any more.

And men will not understand us — for the generation that
grew up before us, though it has passed these years with us
here, already had a home and a calling; now it will return to its
old occupations, and the war will be forgotten — and the generation that has grown up after us will be strange to us and
push us aside. We will be superfluous even to ourselves, we
will grow older, a few will adapt themselves, some others will
merely submit, and most will be bewildered; — the years will
pass by and in the end we shall fall into ruin.[3]

The Breakdown of Morale in Western Europe:
The Brutalization of the Western Character

Since man always understands the Divine at least partially
under the symbol of human personality, it is to be expected
that a change in the human character will produce a change in
mankind's idea of God. Such a change in the Western European concept of God is precisely what took place immediately
after World War I. On the one hand, there was the extremely
negative movement of sensitive personalities away from the
church, and the increasing alienation of the working classes
who saw the church as a symbol of the reactionary classes who
opposed the various socialist movements that arose in France
and Germany as well as in Eastern Europe. On the other hand,
there was the positive reaction of the theologians of crisis, Karl

Barth and his associate, Emil Brunner.[4] Barth reacted strongly against the so-called liberal theology of the prewar period which had identified Christianity with the highest aspirations of Western culture. Barth's famous *Commentary on the Epistle to the Romans* [5] first appeared in 1918 and immediately provoked a storm of praise and criticism, especially from other concerned Christian leaders such as Bultmann and Tillich. Barth was still a parish pastor when he first published his book, but the publicity he received brought about his call as professor of reformed theology at the University of Göttingen in 1921.[6] Barth's first edition of *Romans* showed a great dependence upon the radical Christianity of Kierkegaard and contained much that was indebted to existential philosophy. However, Barth continued his reaction against liberal thought and in 1922 brought out a completely rewritten version of his *Commentary* in which he removed all references to existential philosophy. Barth's chief contribution was his emphasis upon the study of the Bible in and for itself without reading the Bible through the colored glasses of a contemporary philosophical view. He also revived serious interest in the theology of the Reformation period and began the Renaissance of Luther's studies that later grew to embrace the study of Calvin. Barth's emphasis was that God is God, and altogether different from all things human, even from human religion and human culture. This stress on the wholly otherness of God, who cannot be known through a natural revelation such as might be gained through a philosophy of religion, set Barth apart from the concerned liberal theologians who emerged into prominence in the 1920's. Barth had learned early much from existential philosophy, but turned against it and all other philosophy as an idolatrous means of projecting God in man's own image. Barth thus stood for an antirational view of religion that sees man as helpless in spiritual matters, and can only receive the revelation of this completely unknown God which is thrown into history like a stone. One might say that this gospel Barth speaks of is thrown into man's experience more like a surd than a stone. A man can deal with a stone, for he can weigh it and analyze it. He cannot deal with a surd, except to recognize its irrelevance and to reject it. If God is completely unknown except as he reveals himself in the specialized and localized sense that Barth has in mind — that is, through the Scriptures — then this God is really of no concern to man. If God is removed from the world by an impassable difference so that there is no way to him through philosophy or piety, then in a rather strict sense this God is dead to the world or at the least the world is dead to him. It is not an accident that William Hamilton shows such a heavy Barthian influence in his radical writings, or that Altizer can speak of Barth as contributing to the modern situation in which it is possible to speak of the death of God. The utterly transcendent God of Barth, never really surpassed by his later development of the "humanity of God," is really defined out of existence for man just as effectively as the extreme secularists' assessment of God defined him out of existence by thinking of God as an illusion.

It is therefore quite to the point to treat the rise of Barth's theology in connection with the historical circumstances that helped bring it to birth. The breakdown of Western man's morale was not to be corrected by the new theology, although elements of the new theology were to provide some structure for the continuance of the Christian tradition in middle Europe through the turmoils of the 1920's and 1930's and was to give some comfort to the ineffective efforts of the church to resist Nazism.

What had happened to the European mentality after the 1914–1918 experiences was the complete erosion of the belief that kindness and tolerance were stronger than brutality and self-seeking. Not only the victories in battle, brought about not so much by the greater justice of the winning side as by the greater amounts of money and manpower of the victors, but the utter cynicism of the peace treaties underscored the virtue of strength and the usefulness of brutality. The sense of the utter uselessness of the Christian virtues was deepened by the continuing struggles that racked Russia, Poland, and other European states. The general international war was followed by continuing civil wars in many nations. In these struggles, particularly the decade-long civil strife in the USSR, the various Allied nations took one side or the other in view of whatever benefit might accrue to them rather than out of a sense that either the Whites or the Reds were right. This cynicism was not lost upon the two strata of society that had been alienated from the church since the early portion of the nineteenth century, the intellectuals and the depressed working classes.[7]

The Failure of Protestant and Roman Catholic Moralism to Cope with the Problems of the Twentieth Century

The cleavage between the mind of European man and his spirit was intensified by the utter lack of insight of the bishops and the councils of the Protestant and Catholic churches throughout the period of Europe's turmoil, 1914 to the present. The Protestant churches, rather than seeing the applicability of Jesus' teaching to the legitimate demands of the poor and the dispossessed, reaffirmed, unconsciously if not consciously, their alliance with the reactionary forces that continued to hold control of the parliaments and industries of Europe. Very few of the Christian leaders saw the alienated intellectuals and working classes as the true field for evangelization, but held to the villages and the middle class and rejected the claims of humanity in favor of the rights of propriety and property. It thus came about that the rising political movements that were destined later to control the parliaments of most European states, the socialists and left-wing organizations of various kinds, were confirmed as enemies of the established churches rather than becoming the natural allies they could, and on occasion did become. In Germany, where the extreme elements of socialist revolution were defeated, and more moderate groupings came to the fore, a small group of Christian intellectuals attempted a mediating task between the socialists and the resources of Christianity. This group, the spokesman of which was the young war veteran and university professor Paul Tillich, never really had a chance at the exercise of political power. Its chief accomplishment was the production of the soul-searching studies made by Tillich and others, and the influence it had upon the social thinking of Christian leaders in America (such as Reinhold Niebuhr) and the leaders of other governments decades later. The churches held to their time-honored tradition of subservience to the powers that be, and refused to cooperate with the forward-looking intellectuals who still loved the church. The people by and large did not support this movement any better than they supported modern Germany's first attempt to establish Anglo-Saxon-like democracy (the Weimar Republic), and the extremists who saw religion only as a tool to be used or an enemy to be suppressed, triumphed in 1933. In one last desperate attempt to foster religious socialism against the brutality of national socialism, Tillich published *The Socialist Decision* [8] in 1933. That year Hitler came to power and his first act was to remove Tillich and all other intellectual opponents from their posts. Karl Barth, himself a socialist, was forced to return to Switzerland, and all those who felt their responsibilities to God and/or man either fled or were imprisoned.

These incidents only typify the failure of the church to respond creatively to the rise of a political consciousness among the masses, and to the changed conditions of modern life. Such incidents might be multiplied endlessly, with examples given from England and America as well as from the Continent. And this era of blindness on the part of the church or at least of many of the church's leaders and people is by no means at an end. In America, it was the solid Anglo-Saxon middle classes who resisted the rise of labor organizations, of civil rights groups, and of modern social legislation. In the sixth decade

of the twentieth century, in the South and other areas of the
United States, many times it is pastors and church people who
still resist the organization of labor and the full integration of
all social groups into the life of the community and the church.
It is no accident that the names given to many extremely conservative organizations contain the word " Christian," and that
such utterly irreligious movements as the Ku-Klux Klan claim
to exist in order to reestablish a " Christian America." Although
the leadership of the American churches and many of their
members are much more sensitive to human problems and progressive in their outlook than were the churches of Europe
forty years ago, the church has become so widely identified
with reaction that it does not seem ridiculous to millions in
America, South Africa, and elsewhere to identify Christianity
with the self-identity of one race. The attitude of the church
itself, and its identification of the point of transcendence in
life with the highest aspirations of the people among whom it
was set, is the acid that led to the breakdown of the piety and
reestablished theology of the scholarly believers that we have
called the great synthesizers.

*Internal Influences That Led to the Divorce of the Western
Mind and Spirit*

While millions of Europeans and increasing numbers of
Americans came to recognize the irrelevance of the traditional
churches and their doctrines to the problems of war and social
justice posed by the twentieth century, and thousands more
embraced the essentially reactionary theology of the Barthian
movement, a third group of sensitive individuals both within
and without the church increasingly evolved a Protestant social
consciousness. The rise of human sensitivity to the needs of
others is one of the bright spots in any survey of the history of
our century. This growth of humanitarianism was by no means
limited to the Protestant churches, but included Catholic Christians, believing and secular Jews, and people who were

estranged from all forms of religion. In the churches, this so-cial consciousness was early reflected in the organization of in-terdenominational and international groups that sought to alleviate the distress caused by World War I, and the wars that followed it. Various relief organizations came into being that distributed food and clothing to the needy from Germany to China. The International Red Cross experienced a large growth, and this growing social consciousness found political expression in the League of Nations and other organizations dedicated to the maintenance of peace and the upbuilding of man.

The international community of sensitive men was dealt a severe blow by the victory of the conservative forces in Amer-ica which prevented the participation of the United States in the League of Nations. The League of Nations and the hopes of a growing number of churchmen in Scandinavia, England, and America for a progressive movement that would seek to eliminate the causes of social disorder and war were all dashed to pieces on the intransigence of the reactionary forces that desired to keep America out of the affairs of the rest of the world, and the growing militant nationalism of Germany, Italy, Japan, and other states. In an almost inverse way the churches, or at least a progressive vanguard of churchmen, and the national leaders of Europe proceeded along different pathways. The various Protestant denominations grew closer together — a movement that was later to culminate in the or-ganization of the World Council of Churches. The nations of the world, on the other hand, tended to pull apart, and each sought its own national interest — a movement that ended in the Japanese invasion of China, civil war in Spain, and the Italian adventures in Africa. These crises led to the death of the League and the utter disillusionment of many socially con-cerned persons. The advent of a general worldwide economic depression in the 1930's only served to aggravate these larger problems and forced many sensitive people into an unwise embrace of Communism.

These external events led to the internalization of divisive forces in many members of the church. In America, Reinhold Niebuhr began his prophetic work of calling for a more progressive social attitude on the part of the church and called for resistance to the Fascism that had begun to predominate in central Europe. In this work of calling the churches and the people of the West to rise up against Nazism, which plunged the world into war in 1939, Niebuhr affected the thinking of tens of thousands of clergymen and church members. During World War II and for a decade afterward, Niebuhr's neo-orthodoxy was to be the prevailing theology of most church leaders and many of the clergy.

In Europe, beginning in the 1930's, a group of churchmen arose who more or less shared the social concerns of Tillich and Niebuhr, but who were more orthodox than either. This group was to dignify the Christian name by being the only organized group that sought to oppose Hitler in Germany after 1933. The leaders of this " Confessing Church " movement included Martin Niemoeller, Hanns Lilje, and — although he was quite young — Dietrich Bonhoeffer (1906–1945). The chief inspiration for this movement which sought to prevent the church's being used by the state for its own purposes was Karl Barth. The clergymen and laymen who met in Barmen in 1934 to draft the Barmen Declaration were mainly individuals who had been moved by Barth's theological works to desire a return to a Biblical theology and a distinction between Christianity and the culture in which they lived. The Barmen Declaration began: " Jesus Christ, such as Scripture bears witness of Him for us, is the one word of God that we must hear, that we must trust, and that we must obey in life and death." Of course the opposition of the few Christians that supported the Confessing Church was not enough to overcome the entrenched power of national socialism. The leaders, Niemoeller, Lilje, Otto Dibelius, and the youthful theologian Bonhoeffer, along with hundreds of others, were imprisoned and some suffered martyrdom. This effort, however, as feeble as it was, was a sign that the church was desperately trying to join the modern world. Most of the members of the Confessing Church would only bear witness to their faith by speaking out, but a few, like Bonhoeffer, the Count von Moltke, the Count Stauffenberg, and others, drawn from both wings of the German Protestant Church, from the Roman Catholic Church, and from the remnants of the Democratic Socialist movement, attempted to bring the war to a conclusion by the assassination of Hitler. This attempt also failed, but it too marks a turning point in the attitude of European Christians toward the problems that plagued the twentieth century.[9]

After the tragedy of World War II ended, the theologians who had served the Confessing Church became the leaders of the church in Germany, and the prestige of the neo-orthodoxy of Barth and Niebuhr reached its height. The modern world had weathered another storm and it appeared that the church had weathered the crisis also. In America the age of religiosity arrived, and the churches experienced their greatest increase in growth in the history of the republic. Church attendance was good, and by and large the neo-orthodox sermons of the clergy were well received. The world went back to normal, now on a higher standard of living, for, thanks to war production, the economic depression had been overcome. In the general atmosphere of relief that the war was over, and the optimism generated by the vast increase in scientific technology brought about by the war, the American people apparently had no deep theological doubts about God or his goodness. In Europe this same optimism was fostered by a rapid recovery of both the victorious and the vanquished states that saw increases in living standards on all sides by the end of the first decade of peace. And yet, only ten or twelve years later the church finds itself faced with the announcement of "the death of God." This startling symbol of the complete separation of the mind and spirit is being used, as it turns out, not by individuals who suffered through the depression and the war, but in the main by men who have come to maturity since 1945. What is the explanation? Why did the transitory fame garnered for the church by leaders like the German bishops and Niebuhr fade so quickly? Why is it true that we find an inverse relationship between the financial and membership situations of the church and the innermost beliefs of the people at large? How do we explain the appeal of the radical theology of Hamilton and Altizer among the student population in concert with the continued popularity of a completely undemythologized and simplistic gospel like that proclaimed by Billy Graham?

The answers to the above questions are not readily discernible, but some of the elements of the answers are not hard to identify. In the first place, there was no real demonstration of the strength of Christianity in the crisis of World War II. People who most courageously resisted the dictators found themselves with little in the Christian tradition to draw on except the willingness of the historical Jesus to go to the cross. It is a fact that the one creative theologian of the Confessing Church, Bonhoeffer, found it necessary to project a religionless Christianity. He found that the church as it existed was not capable of resisting tyranny of either the philosophical or political variety. Bonhoeffer found that the church as an institution was not capable of practicing and proclaiming Christianity. He came to the same conclusion, as Kierkegaard had almost a century before, that the antithesis of Christianity was Christendom.

Secondly, the problems that led to the terrors and hardships of revolutions, depressions, and world wars were not settled by the military victories of the West. The world did not enter an era of peace after 1945, but, as it became quite clear in 1947, had entered a twilight era of struggle between the Western nations and the Soviet bloc which Churchill called the "Cold War." The underlying problems of the century erupted again and again into external violence. In 1950–1953, the conflict in Korea caused a widening breach between East and West and added another million casualties to the century's total. Year by

year other conflicts arose in Africa, the Middle East, Asia, and
Latin America. In Indo-China, the end of the world war sig-
naled the beginning of the Vietnamese war which continues to
the date of this writing. In short, as the years passed, men and
women everywhere began to see that there was nothing new
under the sun and although everything had changed, ex-
ternally, everything remained the same. One cannot understand
the present climate of spiritual opinion in Europe and America
without reference to the growing sense of frustration and the
increasing repulsiveness of the actions of both " Christian "
and " atheistic " nations on the part of the normally idealistic
younger generations.

In America, another problem forced the split between mind
and spirit to the fore in the minds of the young. This was the
century-old, but not yet settled problem of the integration of
eighteen million citizens of the Negro race into the social
fabric of the nation. The civil rights movement began among
the young, has been carried through chiefly by men and women
who have come to maturity since the end of World War II,
and is even now being carried on by people in thier twenties.
This movement has deep roots in the American character as
well as in the American experience. It was the issue of slavery
that helped to shape the destiny of the American nation in the
nineteenth century, a destiny that had to be reached by passing
through the crucible of a terrible civil war. The American character, shaped as it has been by the belief in liberty and by an
often-unfounded confidence in the ability of the individual to
better himself when given the opportunity, could no longer remain indifferent to the denial of liberty and opportunity to
Negro citizens. Thus the civil rights movement experienced an
influx of strength from the idealistic student generation. This
movement gave them a cause for which to live which seem-
ingly could be brought to a victorious conclusion in their own
lifetime. Here was a worthwhile thing to do which could be
engaged in and from which life could derive interest and

meaning. In the seminaries where liberal thought was permitted or encouraged, the movement came as a salutary influence to fill the vacuum left by the obviously inadequate orthodox theology that many of the students could not accept.

The movement to advance human rights was and remains attractive to all persons impressed by the residual elements of the liberal theological proclamation of the life and teaching of the historical Jesus. It is quite understandable that creative theological thinkers since World War II have turned to a description of Jesus in terms of his function as a healer, friend of man, and inspirer of selfless action. This "functional Christology" has been developed in a relatively traditional way by the preacher-poet Joseph Sittler, of the University of Chicago, and in a radical way by William Hamilton, of Colgate Rochester Divinity School.[10] Hamilton speaks of Jesus in the words of Bonhoeffer as a "man for others" and says that Jesus for us is "a place to be." For Hamilton, and for hundreds of socially concerned students, many of them theological students, the place to be that is Jesus-like is in the civil rights movement in Mississippi or in northern urban slums.

The change of viewpoint concerning the person and work of Jesus Christ is part of the configuration of ideas that has developed within the Christian church since World War II. Long before our present period we had philosophers and cultural leaders who valued Jesus as a symbol and as the highest expression of what man ought to be, while these same thinkers paid little attention to belief in God. George Santayana (1863–1952) is famous for his remark, "There is no God and Mary is his mother." Santayana in his *Interpretations of Poetry and Religion* [11] writes of the power of the preaching of Paul, a proclamation that Santayana says consists in one thing: "Christ and Him crucified." Santayana explains the power of Christ in words that are applicable to the present situation, which has been characterized by the pun: "There is no God, and Jesus is his only begotten son."

"Therein was a new poetry, a new ideal, a new God. Therein was the transcript of the real experience of humanity, as men found it in their inmost souls and as they were dimly aware of it in universal history. The moving power was a fable — for who stopped to question whether its elements were historical, if only its meaning were profound and its inspiration contagious? This fable had points of attachment to real life in a visible brotherhood and in an extant worship, as well as in the religious past of a whole people. At the same time it carried the imagination into a new sphere; it sanctified the poverty and sorrow at which Paganism had shuddered; it awakened tenderer emotions, revealed more human objects of adoration, and furnished subtler instruments of grace. It was a whole world of poetry descended among men, like the angels at the Nativity, doubling, as it were, their habitation, so that they might move through supernatural realms in the spirit while they walked the earth in the flesh. The consciousness of new loves, new duties, fresh consolations, and luminous unutterable hopes accompanied them wherever they went. They stopped willingly in the midst of their business for recollection, like men in love; they sought to stimulate their imaginations, to focus, as it were, the long vistas of an invisible landscape." [12]

This is a completely naturalistic explanation of the power of Christ, but one that values, as we would expect a poet to value, the power of myth over the mind of man. Jesus is the ideal of humanity, the picture of what the sensitive and socially concerned person ought to be. In the relevantly flat language of Hamilton, we have a kind of minimal evaluation of the Lordship of Jesus.[13] Although we may feel that Hamilton's development of Bonhoeffer's emphasis on Jesus' weakness [14] and other-directedness is a one-sided presentation of Christology, we cannot but affirm that Jesus certainly was this kind of individual. Bishop John A. T. Robinson has developed the theme of Christology as functional analysis of Jesus' other-directedness in the popular work *Honest to God*,[15] devoting a chapter to the discussion of " Christmas and Truth." E. L. Mascall [16] has written a lengthy critique of Robinson's rather loosely organized pamphlet, going on to criticize Paul van Buren's *Secular Meaning of the Gospel* [17] as well. Mascall, an orthodox Anglo-Catholic, has no sympathy for either of the radical theologians and attempts to pick their arguments to pieces in the apparent hope that his readers will conclude that such a mass of negative assessments has refuted the arguments of his opponents. Such is not the case, for Mascall is of a mind set that feels that a position is refuted when it has been shown to be unorthodox. Actually, Mascall's book is quite helpful if one reads it open-mindedly, for he points out the connection of the radical theology with the historic liberal theology that forms part of the contrapuntal tradition. Mascall will say openly what many liberal writers only say guardedly, and he correctly assesses the Christology of Robinson and other radical thinkers to amount to this: " The divinity of Jesus Christ is his perfect humanity. That is the conscious or unconscious status of modern Christology in almost every representative thinker." [18]

Thus we may understand the career of Christology in the twentieth century as part of the internal influence that has contributed to the breakdown of the remnants of the orthodox theology — and increasingly of the traditional polity — of the Christian church. The development of a functional Christology which stresses Jesus' humanity could not be avoided because it is the natural result of the piety of Wilhelm Herrmann, the mysticism of Schweitzer, and the correlative existentialism of Tillich. This stress on Jesus as human being is a natural outgrowth of the general acceptance of Bultmann's program of demythologization of the New Testament, which has even begun to make a small impression on Barth, who in recent years has turned to a discussion of the humanity of God.[19]

In this chapter we have briefly surveyed the elements of twentieth-century thought and experience that have contributed to the breakup of modern man's mind, in the sense of his rational acceptance of theological doctrines, and his spirit, which longs for the increase of peace, cooperativeness, and sensitivity among men. We have seen that the harsh external realities of war, and reactionary leadership in the churches which has prevented a clear-cut identification of the Christian ethic with liberal social democracy, has led to the conclusion on the part of many that the church is irrelevant to modern life. We have also seen that the internal development of a social consciousness among many churchmen has led to their involvement in political affairs, and has quite naturally influenced younger theologians to begin to define the doctrine of Christ in terms of the historical Jesus as a symbol of human social concern. The twentieth century, by and large, has lived on the grace that was mediated by the great synthesizers, Herrmann, Schweitzer, Bultmann, and Tillich, but their influence has not actually changed the structure of the church itself. The rise of idealistic and liberal piety in these scholarly representatives has not been enough to offset the concomitant rise of reaction and revolution in our time. There is still a chance that the liberal piety of reverence for life which has become such a constructive element in the civil rights movement through the genius of Martin Luther King may point the way toward a more Christlike social order in the future. However, the forces of reaction are at work among the younger Negro leaders today, and the principle of nonviolence may yet be rejected by those who have benefited from its use. In short, the old framework of a Christian society has broken up, but fragments of it are preserved and used as weapons for the maintenance of power in such areas as the South and among conservatives in all parts of the world. This fact lends urgency to the call of Bonhoeffer for a religionless Christianity. A Christianity that expresses itself in personal relationships and in built-in safeguards for human dignity and welfare in every society is the ultimate aim of those who see Jesus as the man for others. This movement toward a Christlike attitude toward men is the ultimate aim of the Protestant belief in the possibility of living sacredly in the secular realm. It is not a heresy or a denial of the Christianity of the Gospels which portrayed Jesus as paying Caesar's tax and going about doing good. The man who most clearly saw the need for a worldly Christianity outlined some of these things while in prison. This man, who has become the symbol of the radically serious Christian thought of our time, Bonhoeffer, hoped to write a book about the real meaning of the Christian faith, but was killed by the demonic forces of the twentieth-century moral breakdown before he could do so. He wrote:

Our relation to God [is] not a religious relationship to a supreme Being, absolute in power and goodness, which is a spurious conception of transcendence, but a new life for others, through participation in the Being of God. The transcendence consists not in tasks beyond our scope and power, but in the nearest thing to hand. God in human form, not, as in other religions, in animal form — the monstrous, chaotic, remote and terrifying — nor yet in abstract form — the absolute, metaphysical, infinite, etc. — nor yet in the Greek divine-human of autonomous man, but man existing for others, and hence the Crucified.[20]

For Bonhoeffer, the reality of God is not made manifest in the church in any way other than it is made manifest in the secular world. God is to be known not only in the church, but in the family, in our work, and in the governments of man. God's commandments are not such as to call us to live as something other than men, but actually demand that we live as men responsible for the institutions of which we are a part. Although no one can say how Bonhoeffer would have developed his thought, had he lived, it seems clear that those who see in his literary remains a mandate for participation in political life, in the civil rights movement, and in the various movements that aim to end the involvement of nations in war, are correctly reading what was closest to Bonhoeffer's heart. The heart of Bonhoeffer's theology, as inadequate as it may be, is the same as the Christology of Hamilton, Altizer, and other radical thinkers today: "The earthly form of Christ is the form that died on the cross. . . . But when a man follows Jesus Christ and bears the image of the incarnate, crucified and risen Lord, when he has become the image of God, we may at last say that he has been called to be the ' imitator of God.' The follower of Jesus is the imitator of God." [21]

We may conclude this discussion of the breakdown of Western morale and the separation of the Western mind and spirit by saying that the almost complete dissolution of the orthodox traditional cultural framework due to World War I and the withering away of the orthodox content of theology since the eighteenth century has resulted in the era of the "death of God." In our lifetime we have witnessed the collapse of most of the props of the traditional doctrine of God and the clear emergence of a humanistic evaluation of Jesus. We might say that we have passed through the experience of the death of the Divine and of the ideological resurrection of the historical — and purely human — Jesus.

Chapter V
The Rise of the Radicals

T HE SPIRITUAL experience of the last decade we have termed the death of the Divine and the resurrection of the historical, human Jesus. Such an experience has been brought about by the appearance of certain rather radical religious thinkers and has provoked the rise of other radical commentators. The various internal and external influences on the breakup of Protestant scholarly piety have served to form the stance of these radical thinkers, but we must beware of the Marxist deterministic fallacy, for these thinkers have freely and courageously reacted to their spiritual environment. Mircea Eliade (1907–   ) has observed that the influences of economic and cultural factors on ideologies does not annul the objective value of these ideologies any more than the fever or intoxication that reveals a new poetic creation to a poet impairs the value of that creation.[1] If we have given the impression up to now that everything is determined for man by large, historymaking forces, this chapter will serve as a corrective, for we now turn to a descriptive critique of those thinkers who have pioneered modern radical Christianity.

A Brief Description of the " God Is Dead " Theologians

The sixth decade of the twentieth century has witnessed the rise of several young theologians who have advocated the most radical views in their interpretations of the Christian faith.

The thinking of these young theologians has been labeled by the press as "the death of God" movement. The major figures of this movement are Thomas J. J. Altizer, Paul van Buren, and William Hamilton. A fourth figure often associated with this group is Gabriel Vahanian, a sociologist of religion who popularized the phrase "the death of God" by entitling a book concerning the American religious situation with this phrase.[2]

The most prominent of the "death of God" theologians is Thomas J. J. Altizer (1928–   ), an associate professor of religion in the undergraduate college at Emory University. Altizer was educated at the University of Chicago under the famous historian of religion Joachim Wach. Altizer's field of competence is Buddhism, with particular reference to Oriental mysticism. Altizer has published three books alone and a fourth in collaboration with William Hamilton.[3] Altizer has brought the movement that he calls the new or radical theology into public notice by his unique style and flair for unusual statements. He has written:

"We must recognize that the death of God is a historical event: God has died in *our* time, in *our* history, in *our* existence. Insofar as we live in our destiny, we can know neither a trace of God's presence nor an image of his reality."[4]

Altizer is almost incomprehensible to most people because he represents a point of view so utterly opposed to the usual or orthodox preaching of the church. But as we have seen from our survey of the contrapuntal tradition, this is no indication that he is wrong. Although his position looks iconoclastic, he is actually seeking (although we might admit in a confused way) to expound a positive message that he feels is needed by the church today. Altizer seeks to help man rediscover the realities that are represented by the symbols of God and other church doctrines in the values of the secular world itself. He has become aware of a general breakdown of belief in God among Western men. He feels that we have arrived at a point in history where men are completely secular. Although some men may speak of the things of religion, they do not necessarily believe in religion or live by its principles. Altizer has assumed the stance of a prophet, one that fits him well, for he is a layman, as were most of the Hebrew prophets. Many times the Divinity School at Emory University is attacked for having Altizer on its faculty, but this is a misunderstanding, for Altizer has no connection with the Methodist Seminary which is located on the Emory University campus.

Altizer is something of a mystic and a poet who has been greatly influenced not only by Joachim Wach but also by Mircea Eliade, the historian of religion presently at the University of Chicago. Altizer says that he is looking for a " coincidence of opposites," which means that he is looking for a rediscovery of the sense of the sacred in the midst of man's secularity. Thus Altizer declares that the older version of religion (that is, of the sacred) is forever past, that " God is dead," for the sacred cannot be found by looking backward to a prior epoch in man's history when the sacred was found in the church and in the symbols associated with belief in a transcendent God. For Altizer, in his radical reassessment of religion, the secular is now for us really the sacred. He seems to believe that if modern men follow his advice, God will "resurrect himself" out of the midst of man's secular vision of the world. In simple language, this means that man will find God in this world, under our modern forms of thought.

In 1966, Altizer published his latest work, *The Gospel of Christian Atheism,* a record of the most radical development of his thought. It is to be expected that the book will be greeted by loud denunciations from many theologians and by extravagant praise from the more radical sector of modern thinkers. In this work, Altizer declares that Christianity now confronts the most radical challenge that it has faced since it began. According to Altizer, the church is not equipped to face this challenge and the Christian theologian today must work completely outside the framework and the theological thought

forms of the organized church. Altizer says there is no reason
why Christianity should be identified with its ecclesiastical expressions; indeed, much of the trouble in which the church
finds itself — and in which Christianity seems to be — is due to
the false identification of Christianity with the Christian
church. Altizer calls for theologians with the courage and faith
to recognize and celebrate the fact that we are living in a
post-Christian age. No longer is theology tied to the church,
for the first duty of the Christian theologian must be seen
as, not loyalty to the church, but loyalty to Christ, that is,
loyalty to Christ as he is met in the totality of human experience.

William Hamilton (1925–   ) is a young Baptist theologian
teaching at Colgate Rochester Divinity School. Prior to becoming the radical thinker he now is, he produced several
helpful studies on the New Testament. His background is that
of the older Protestant neo-orthodoxy. While Altizer is influenced by Tillich and Eliade, Hamilton is heavily influenced by
the great American social gospel tradition. This can be seen
in his emphasis upon Christ as an example for interpersonal
relationships and his reduction of Christianity to Christlike
ethics. His radical thought stems from his reading of the French
existentialists Albert Camus and Jean-Paul Sartre. He first expressed his views in the book *The New Essence of Christianity* [5] in which he holds that men no longer are able to accept
belief in a transcendent deity or to believe in traditional theology. Thus the theologian must "reduce the area of belief
and lay hold on those few things of which we can be certain." [6]
Those few things include our obligation to love one another
and to recognize the tragic situation in which modern man
finds himself. Hamilton agrees with Camus who wrote that it
is better to give a cup of milk to a child in need than to say a
million Masses. Hamilton declares that the modern experience
of "the death of God" (that is, one's experiences of depending
on science for the solution of problems and not on God) now

summons man to follow Jesus, who was a "man for others" — a truly good man, who lived only for the good that he could do for other men. Christians today are to be about their work of doing "Jesus things" and showing love to a war-torn world. In this ethical assessment, no genuine Christian could demur, yet the theology behind it seems very shallow.

Hamilton is greatly influenced by the young Lutheran martyr and theologian Dietrich Bonhoeffer, who was killed by the Nazis. This influence, combined with Hamilton's social gospel influence, explains his reduction of Christianity to ethics and the honoring of the "historical Jesus." Hamilton has changed his view several times in the last few years and seems to be getting more radical with each publication. His work exhibits a certain confusion also. It is not clear, for example, whether Hamilton thinks that God is simply absent and will soon reappear, whether God never really existed, or whether God somehow has died.

Paul van Buren (1925–) formerly taught at the Episcopal Seminary of the Southwest in Austin, Texas. Since publishing his book *The Secular Meaning of the Gospel*,[7] he has given up theology and moved to the philosophy department at Temple University, Philadelphia. Basically, van Buren is a language philosopher. In his book, he applied the techniques of philosophical analysis to the creeds of the church and to the New Testament. After doing this, he concluded that "any language about God as being alive or dead is meaningless."[8] In this assessment, van Buren reveals his own ignorance of the development of language philosophy, for while the earlier linguistic analysis would have come to a similar conclusion, the newer ordinary language philosophy would not. Ordinary language would see theological language as perfectly meaningful among believers, while the earlier language philosophers would have judged theological language by standards appropriate only to physics or biology. Van Buren says that once we see that "God language" is symbolic, we will see that when it is analyzed nothing is left for us to believe or reject. He implies that modern men are quite able to live without the God hypothesis. We do not need God to meet our needs or solve our problems, for we have modern science to solve our problems for us.

Van Buren, like Hamilton, proceeds to reduce Christianity to admiration for the "historical Jesus" who was a kind, unselfish man, open to the problems of other men. We Christians today ought to follow Jesus' example, for in such loving conduct life could be far better than it is living by other standards, according to van Buren.

Karl Barth: Catalyst of Radical Thought

Despite the adornment of page after page of "radical" theological articles with the name of Dietrich Bonhoeffer, a serious effort at disentangling the ideas developed in the writings of Hamilton and Altizer discloses the dependence of each upon the thought of Paul Tillich and Karl Barth. Beneath the veneer of the Nietzschean phraseology and the illustrative materials drawn from Camus, Kafka, Herman Melville, William Blake, and Bonhoeffer,[9] the framework of the newly emerged radical theology is a blend of thoughts that bear an ambiguous relation to Barth's "wholly other" theism and a fairly direct relation to Tillich's "ecstatic naturalism" and existentialist analysis of the human condition. Indeed, so pervasive is Barth's influence on Hamilton and Altizer that we might speak of the Swiss theologian as the reluctant father of their thought, if it were not the case that the young radicals have drawn conclusions from Barth's insights that are antithetical to Barth's own. It is necessary to point out this ambiguous relationship to Barth so that the rather direct influence of Tillich (discussed below) will become clearer. To show Barth's contribution to the radical theology we need mention only two salient factors: (1) Barth was the major influence on the symbolic figure of religionless Christianity, Bonhoeffer [10]; and (2) Barth is the

author of an essay on the work of the nineteenth-century posi-
tivist, Ludwig Feuerbach.[11]

Barth's greatest contribution to theology is his emphasis upon
the disunity of the natural and the divine. With the advent of
his thought, the pendulum of modern theology swung back
from the humanistic liberalism of Harnack, Ritschl, and Herrmann to a stress on the majesty and transcendence of God.

William Hamilton has placed Barth squarely in the middle of
the problems that Hamilton believes have given rise to the experience of "the death of God." Hamilton says that Barth
gives us a correct doctrine of God in his writings. Barth's view
is that God reveals himself to us in the Bible and holds that we
cannot know God in any other way except through a response
to that revelation. This is undoubtedly the mainstream Christian view that runs from Augustine to Luther to Barth and includes all the constructive theological systems in Christian
history.[12]

However, Hamilton goes on to say that the content of the
Scriptural revelation has lost its power to influence men in
our era. Hamilton writes: "I am convinced that the most
serious leakage caused by this traditional and correct portrait
of God today is at the point of the problem of suffering. There
is something in this correct doctrine of God that keeps it from
dealing responsibly with the problem, and therefore, because of this silence and carelessness, one can claim today that
the problem of suffering has become a major barrier to faith
for many sensitive unbelievers." [13]

Hamilton then discusses the treatment of the problem of
evil by Camus in his novel, *The Plague*.[14] He concludes that
Camus' sensitivity to the suffering of children is more acceptable to the modern consciousness than is the arbitrary answer
to the problem of evil found in orthodox theology. Hamilton
thus suggests that sensitive men today reject belief in the
"orthodox God."

Hamilton's whole book, as well as his other writings,[15] pre-

supposes the absence of God. Hamilton is difficult to understand on this basic point, for he does not give us any criteria
by which to measure the presence or absence of God other
than pointing out that: "The experiences of many men in our
time have suggested that the traditional sovereign and omnip-
otent God is a difficult God to perceive or to meet." [16] This
is, of course, a severe critique of the neo-orthodoxy established
by Karl Barth.

Hamilton is very clear in his delineation of the radical position as being polarized negatively on the theological approach
of Barth. He is quite frank in his essay "Thursday's Child," [17]
saying that the theologian in America is a man without faith
and therefore without God. He describes the so-called American theologian as a man who doesn't believe in God, for he
has trouble understanding what man can mean by speaking of
"God." This modern theologian no longer goes to church, since
he finds the life of the church banal. He does not write books
in systematic theology after getting his dissertation published,
or else the books he writes are books for his colleagues that
express the difficulties that he experiences. He reads the Bible
only because he makes his living that way, for the Bible is
strange to him, although some parts of it still excite him. Then
Hamilton describes the status of the radical theologian as opposed to Barth, in the place where this opposition is most clear,
one's attitude toward the Bible.

The theologian is alienated from the Bible, just as he is alienated from God and the church. This alienation may not last. If
it doesn't last, fine; if it does last, the theologian will have some
piercing questions to ask of himself. But there are wrong ways
(Karl Barth) and right ways to overcome this alienation, and
for now he has to be honest with himself, with the God before
whom he stands in unbelief, and he must wait.[18]

Hamilton goes on to complete his essay by saying that the
theologian simply lives his life like any other man, although
the modern theologian tends to identify his secular existence

with a genuine understanding of the meaning of the church. The church for him is present wherever Christ is being formed among men in the world. This means that the radical theologian still has strong feelings about the Jesus Christ of the Bible and has decided that while he may not have faith in the sense of sacrificing his intellect to a doctrinal system (which is what he feels the faith of Barth and of the orthodox church really is), and he may not even have hope for the reception of faith in the future, he still has love.[19] This love he sees exemplified in Jesus, which he defines not as a person or as God, but as a standpoint from which to view the life of man. This means that radical theology is a radical ethic of love, which expresses itself in the civil rights movement and in the academic world. Hamilton claims that this image of the modern theologian is consciously modeled on the teaching of Bonhoeffer and ends his essay with the implication that such a style of life is the only honest option open to the theologian today.

Nothing could be farther from the theology of Barth. Yet we cannot escape the conclusion that such a style of life has been formed in conscious opposition to what Hamilton calls "the Augustinian doubt maneuver."[20] Augustine, Hamilton means, overcame his skepticism by observing that even skepticism implies some belief in truth.[21] Hamilton also rejects the teaching of Tillich which holds that "where the spirit is far from our consciousness, where we are unable to pray or to experience any meaning in life, the Spirit is working quietly in the depths of our souls. In the moment when we feel separated from God, . . . we are not left alone."[22] Thus does Hamilton reject the most orthodox segments of Tillich's teaching, because in this regard Tillich sounds like Barth. Barth and the neo-orthodoxy he helped to found is the real enemy Hamilton struggles against. Barth is precisely the opposite of Hamilton, as Hamilton is well aware. In *The Word of God and the Word of Man*,[23] Barth writes:

For a definition of *faith* I go to that place in the gospel where the words are found, "Lord, I believe, help Thou mine unbelief"; and for a definition of *revelation* to a sentence of Luther, "I do not know it and do not understand it, but sounding from above and ringing in my ears I hear what is beyond the thought of man" (Erlangen Ed., 20, 133). Faith and revelation expressly deny that there is any way from man to God and to God's grace, love, and life. Both words indicate that the only way between God and man is that which leads *from* God *to* man.[24]

Hamilton might be understood as a man who has taken Barth too seriously. At least his first book in the radical tradition, *The New Essence of Christianity*, continues to speak of God as absent,[25] implying that there is a God who may return. However, Hamilton has receded from this relatively "soft" interpretation of the meaning of the declaration "God is dead,"[26] to move to the "official" position which he and Altizer have adopted in their most recent work, which holds that there once was a God, but now there is no such God, for God died in the death of Jesus on the cross.[27]

The position of Hamilton and Altizer on the meaning of the phrase "God is dead" is puzzling to the professional theologian, perhaps more puzzling to him than to the layman, for the theologian cannot see how such a symbol hangs together with the other discernible influences at work in the radical theologian's thought. This is the case because the idea that God himself has died in the death of the physical Jesus is not new, but is a rather extreme development of an ancient heresy called "Patripassianism," which maintained that the essence of Christ was the same as the essence of the Father, and therefore the Father suffered in the suffering of the Son. However, the ancient heresy never asserted that the Father "exhausted Himself" in the Son's death, but rather asserted a kind of unitarianism that denied the independent personality of Christ.[28] Thus, Altizer and Hamilton have a new twist to the interpretation of the death of Christ that has not been seen before in theological thought. Altizer speaks of the new position as "a consistent kenotic Christology," [29] but he is in error, for a kenotic Christology refers to a view of the incarnation based on Phil. 2:5-11, which stresses the idea that Christ emptied himself of his divinity when he was born into the world. Actually, a consistent kenotic Christology would hold that the human being Jesus suffered and died on the cross, and would have difficulty in explaining how Jesus' death has a "divine significance" rather than implying that God died when Jesus died. This is a simple but basic point about which both Altizer and Hamilton seem confused. Of all the possible interpretations that might be placed on the phrase "God is dead," the one that these young theologians have chosen is the one that bears the smallest amount of theological freight and seems to reflect confusion or despair or both. The declaration that "God is dead" need not be so trivial in its meaning, as we have seen from our discussion of the history of radical thought, and one would hope that the exponents of "the death of God" will become clearer about the insights they are offering to us in their future work.

Paul Tillich: Reluctant Father of Radical Theology

The unique interpretation of the "death of God" in the young radicals who have arisen in the last ten years of our American church experience seems to define them over against the giant of American theology, Paul Tillich, as well as from the leading Protestant theologian of Europe, Barth. However, such is not the case. Although Tillich, while he lived, was apparently scandalized by Hamilton and Altizer and their strident declaration of the "death of God," he is one of the major influences on Altizer's thought and indeed upon the thought of any theologian presently at work. Altizer is quite clear in his acknowledgment of his debt to Tillich. In his latest book, *The Gospel of Christian Atheism,* he writes:

It was while reading Tillich as an undergraduate that I was
led to an acceptance of the Christian faith, and I have found
that throughout my teaching and study it was Tillich who ex-
cercised the greatest theological influence upon my work.
Among twentieth-century theologians, it was Tillich alone
who made possible a way to a truly contemporary theology.
While I have been forced to resist and oppose Tillich's theological conclusions, I do so with the conviction that they are
not yet radical enough, and with the memory of Tillich's
words to me that the real Tillich is the radical Tillich. Certainly, Tillich is the modern father of radical theology, and
although he did not succeed in founding a Tillichian school
of theology, his influence is felt at most of those points where
theology is now being carried beyond its traditional limits.[30]

But Altizer (and Hamilton) is equally clear about the other
elements of the theological tradition that have influenced the
new position. In *Radical Theology and the Death of God*, we
read:

Radical theology is peculiarly a product of the mid-twentieth
century; it has been initiated by Barth and neo-orthodoxy into
a form of theology which can exist in the midst of the collapse
of Christendom and the advent of secular atheism. It has also
learned from Paul Tillich and Rudolf Bultmann the necessity
for theology to engage in a living dialogue with the actual
world and history which theology confronts.[31]

In summary, we may observe that Altizer and Hamilton,
along with Paul van Buren and Harvey Cox,[32] make up the
leading edge of the recent wave of radical theology and are
unique — if not incomprehensible — in their theological position. Hamilton and Altizer are not Barthians, but they are influenced by Barth to the extent that they have polarized themselves negatively on his theology. They are not Tillichians, as
there is no Tillichian school, and we have seen that both
Hamilton and Altizer have declared themselves to be in dis-
agreement with elements of Tillich's thought. We will turn
now to a discussion of Tillich, however, which will point out

the truth of Altizer's claim that Tillich is the father of radical theology. Before we do that, in order to be precise, let us remind ourselves that the new theologians are not Patripassians, nor do they present a consistent kenotic (self-emptying) Christology.

Paul Tillich was primarily a teacher who said on many occasions that the primary emphasis of his work was to so teach theology that the young men who came to divinity schools would be able to learn of the Christian heritage and to commit themselves to it with integrity. By this, Tillich meant that he wanted to correlate the insights of Christianity with the insights and knowledge found in the modern arts and sciences, so that young ministers and teachers could be both intelligent modern men and ministers of the word. In an expanded sense, this was also the intent of his theology as a whole, the correlation of the problems of man's existence which express themselves as the questions of philosophy, and the answers to those questions found in the resources of the Christian faith.

Paul Tillich has been rejected as too liberal by many Christians who consider themselves conservative or orthodox. An example of such a rejection is the critique by Kenneth Hamilton [33] which voices appreciation for Tillich's effort to create an apologetic for Christianity but rejects Tillich's content as being alien to the gospel. Perhaps the most reasonable suggestion advanced by Hamilton is that Tillich definitely must be understood as a radical thinker, since he embraces positions that have been defined as heretical by the church, but the labeling of Tillich as a heretic misses the point of his work, since his system shifts the emphasis of the various Christian symbols and represents a new creative attempt to speak to the world.[34] Although this writer disagrees with the critique of Tillich made by Hamilton, we must recognize that liberals as well as conservatives agree that Tillich definitely shifts the emphasis of Christian symbols to a new plane in his system. In this respect,

Altizer is correct in saying that the real Tillich is the radical Tillich.

Unlike Altizer and William Hamilton, and unlike Kenneth Hamilton, Tillich cannot be given a label of "conservative" or "radical." Like all deep systematic thinkers who have produced a large corpus of material over a long lifetime, Tillich defies simple analysis. Additionally, Tillich chose as his life-work the exploration of the boundary land between theology and philosophy, religion and culture, Lutheranism and socialism.[35] Tillich, like his teacher Martin Kahler, was a mediating theologian.[36] Tillich aimed to bring an appreciation of the world and its problems to the attention of the church, on the one hand, and aimed to bring a recognition of the need of the men of the world for the insights of the gospel, on the other. He was a "bridge figure," who definitely contained theologically and politically radical ideas (he was an avowed socialist and exponent of the "deliteralization" of the Bible), but he was also the apologist for Christianity who continued to stress the reality of God and the uniqueness of Jesus Christ. Such a man contained both orthodox as well as radical ideas.

The foundation of the claim that Tillich is the father of radical theology lies in his attack on traditional theism and in his nonincarnational Christology. Tillich rejected the personalistic description of God that has predominated in Christian theology since the time of the Bible.[37] Tillich insisted that to define God as a person was idolatrous, since personality contains limitations and if God were only personal, he would be a part of being and not the Ground and Source of Being. Tillich defined God as Being Itself, the Unconditioned, who is the Source of all that exists and on which all things depend. God contains within himself the basis of personality, but he also contains the foundations of the nonpersonal elements of the world as well. Tillich was not adverse to referring to God as personal, as is done by the Biblical writers, if one understands that such language is symbolic. For Tillich, every word spoken about the Divine is a symbol, except for the assertion that God is Being Itself. Only by such an understanding, Tillich declares, can we escape idolatry. However, Tillich meant his symbolic language to be taken as bearing real meaning, for a symbol, in his view, points beyond itself and participates in the reality to which it points. To speak of our language about God as symbolic is not to say that it is merely imaginative, for the symbols refer to real elements (of love, personality, and fatherlikeness) in the Divine itself.

Tillich's Christology has been subjected to severe criticism by more orthodox theologians, particularly Roman Catholic theologians,[38] who voice great appreciation of his system while criticizing it. Essentially, Tillich's Christology sees Jesus as a human being in whom the separation from God, the Ground of man's being, was uniquely overcome. Tillich does not appreciate the traditional incarnational Christology which speaks of God entering into history and taking on flesh. Along with Bultmann and other modern theologians, Tillich sees such language as mythological, and to his way of thinking, more related to the pagan concept of gods taking on human appearance than to the Judeo-Christian concept of monotheism.[39]

Tillich's interpretation of Christology is an ontological one, that is, one that understands Christ as being connected with the Ground of Being, God, who lies behind and beneath the structures of existence. Briefly understood, Tillich teaches that man is "fallen," which means that he is not in a proper relationship to the Ground of his being, and, therefore, exists in anxiety, finitude, and sin. For Tillich's system, Christ is the bearer of the New Being, which is the restorative principle that makes it possible for man to be at least fragmentarily reunited with the Divine Ground. Tillich has been accused of the heresy of Adoptionism, which holds that Christ was a man who earned the right to be the reuniting figure between God and man. Tillich is certainly not guilty of this charge, for he in no place holds that Jesus did anything to earn his Christhood;

rather, Jesus is the Christ in the totality of his being. It is what Christ is, not what he does, that makes him the saving person. Jesus, however, is to be understood as a man, the only true or perfect man that history has seen. Jesus, in Tillich's own idiom, sacrificed that which was Jesus (that is, personal or particular) in himself to that which was Christ (that is, that which was transparent to the divine depths) in him. Jesus could become the Christ, says Tillich, only by taking suffering and death upon himself, because only in that way could he completely participate in existence and by that participation, conquer the estrangement that separates existing beings from God.[40]

It is clear from this brief description of Tillich's unusual approach to Christian symbols that he might well be the inspiration for other unique and even radical interpretations of Christianity. This is precisely what the claim that Tillich is the father of radical theology means. Tillich was one of the few well-equipped and respected theologians of his time who would live in the dangerous situation of the boundary line and go the second mile to attempt to reach the secular world with the message of Christianity. Many theologians, even in modern times, have attempted systematic theologies — that is, have attempted to make a dialogue with the world and have even adopted some of the philosophical and linguistic tools of secular disciplines — to endeavor to make the Christian faith more understandable to secular man. However, none of these theologians have taken the world as seriously as did Tillich. Barth is well known for his expression that the gospel is hurled at man like a stone, and his fellow theologian of crisis, Brunner, who broke with Barth over this attitude, does not really go too far beyond it in his own denial that there can be a legitimate philosophy of religion. Thus Altizer is correct in maintaining that it is Tillich alone who makes it possible for us to work toward a truly contemporary theology that will take into account the elements of modern secular, scientific, and technological culture.

*The Radical Call for the Reunion of Mind and Spirit in a Time
That Is Experiencing "the Death of God"*

In attempting to assess the radical theologians in a positive
way, we are confronted with several inherent difficulties that
go much deeper than the ordinary critiques made of these
theologians by orthodox believers who label them as atheists
or worse. We have no desire to add any surface negative criticism to the millions of words that have been written and
preached against Altizer and his friends. Just the opposite,
because we are seriously convinced that it has been the contrapuntal tradition that has usually proven itself to be the truly
creative element in our culture, we want to point out the
merits of the radical theology insofar as we are able.

First of all, we must recognize that the relationship of
Altizer and Hamilton to Tillich is also a negative one, as we
saw that it was in relation to Barth. However, it is not so negative as in Barth's case, because Altizer and Hamilton only
resist and oppose the method Tillich used and some of his
theological conclusions, not all of them. Tillich is reported to
have said, " I say yes to this movement insofar as it points to
something above the symbolic language concerning God,"
but Tillich is also reported to have said no to the movement
insofar as it abandons all symbolic language about God.[41]
Tillich, as we have seen, believed it to be the theologian's
duty to point to the God above God, the Ground of Being, but
he " believed in " God beyond all question. Once, this writer
heard Tillich reply to a question about the assertion that
God is dead with the counter-question, " How can the Ground
of Being die? " On the other hand, Tillich felt that much of the
Christian speech about God was meaningless or absurd because it had identified God with the cultural values of Western society. He warned theologians long before the rise of the
young radicals that " perhaps . . . you must forget everything
traditional that you have learned about God, perhaps even

that word itself." [42] It is interesting to note that one of the
milder radicals, Harvey Cox, concludes his book *The Secular
City* with a warning similar to Tillich's. Cox says, "This may
mean we shall have to stop talking about God for awhile." [43]
Cox holds that it would be well to declare a moratorium on
God-language in order not to confuse the true God who reveals himself in Christ with the gods of mythology or the
divinities put forward by philosophers.

This is the breaking point between Tillich and the radical
theologians. Tillich will criticize Christian God-language, but
he does so in order to affirm the transcendence of God. He
will do away with the word "God," but certainly not with God
as the final referent of man's ultimate concern and worship.
The young radicals want to do away both with God-language
and with God as the object of faith. As conservative commentators and others have noted, the church could deal with
this easily if the radicals would simply call themselves atheists
and leave "theology" alone. But this is precisely what Altizer,
Hamilton, and van Buren will not do. They want to continue
as Christian theologians, although Altizer and Hamilton now
refer to themselves as "Christian atheists." In particular, all
three of these men emphatically want to keep Jesus, defined as
the man for others, as a place to be, as a model of loving selfless concern, who somehow is present in our world with a contagious power of self-sacrifice and goodness. This is the real
inner problem of the radical theology. As to the relationship
of this movement to Tillich, it seems fair to aver that it is but
an extreme overemphasis of one side of Tillich's thought, the
radical side, with the omission of the balancing conservative
elements that his thought contained. This is legitimate use of
one's sources, for Tillich is now part of the great Christian
tradition, but it is also an indication of the one-sidedness of the
radical theology.

No one has painted the difficulties of trying to do away with
God while keeping Jesus any better than has Langdon P.

Gilkey, of the University of Chicago.[44] Gilkey writes that the radicals say that man does not need God even if there were one, but that they also affirm that Jesus is the rightful Lord over all of human life. He also points out that the radicals see the moral standards of the secular world as valid for Christian men. Here is the inner self-contradiction of the radical position. The radicals are affirming a dual Lordship, that of the secular world and that of Jesus. Gilkey points out that the radicals, following Bonhoeffer, hold that there is no contradiction involved because Jesus sided with the world, accepted it, and suffered for it. However (and here Gilkey scores match point), he declares that "no sane man would assert that this [that is, Jesus'] pattern of loving and self-giving behavior is characteristic of the world as we actually find it. The fact is that the world does not even recognize this standard for its life, let alone follow its lead." [45] This is the problem which the radical theologians are going to have to solve. Even looking at them in the most positive light, we cannot blind ourselves to this problem. The standards of love and self-sacrifice which the young radicals recognize in Jesus, as all Christians recognize them, are simply not the standards of the modern world as a whole and are certainly not the standards of Harvey Cox's "secular city."

We cannot solve the problem of the double standard or dual Lordship that the radicals are now seen to have, but we need not conclude that they will not solve it. It is our contention that the radicals have raised important questions and that we dare not push their protesting voices aside. Undoubtedly some of their protestations are too shrill, and perhaps they do protest too much. But in these men the prophetic, the Protestant, spirit is speaking. When Altizer and his friends tell us that we are living as if there were no God, and that perhaps we should acknowledge that "God is dead," they are not describing private visions, but public experiences that we all share. Hamilton, in particular, sounds like the conscience of most younger theologians (and we suspect of laymen as well) when he witnesses to our life situation as completely secularized living in a "basically desacralized cosmos," even while we are members of the church. These younger theologians are definitely still members of the theological circle, the theological enterprise, because they have the tradition of Western Christendom and the question about God as the object of their ultimate concern. Additionally, the optimism of these men is refreshing, and the courage to be, which they display in spite of the sense of the meaninglessness of life so prevalent in our culture, is a genuine Christian attribute. Even the crux of their problem: Just what can you do with Jesus without God? demonstrates their status as theologians. Each one of these Radicals is completely Christocentric in his thought, revealing the lineal continuity of this movement to the older liberalism. Thus, even if the radicals call themselves Christian atheists, they are still Christian.

What provoked the rise of this excessively radical theology? Why have the young radicals moved so far to the left of Tillich's criticism of theism? We will investigate the elements that provoked the rise of the new theology in the next chapter, but we may mention several considerations here.

The generation that preceded us passed through the experiences of demythologizing the gospel, hoping to recover its inner meaning. But the recovery made by that attempt was not strong enough to last. The problem of our present period is not only that we reject the literalism of religious mythology, which has been done by theologians for decades, but that many men today no longer believe in the meaning of the demythologized myths. This is to say that when the Biblical message is transposed from the myths and symbols in which it was written into a modern mode of discourse such as existentialism, it still is not acceptable or understandable to the average modern man. For a while Tillich was able to cover this problem with his great learning and keen sensitivity to the modern

temper, but not even his ontological theology with its sympathetic approach to both religion and the world is enough to
overcome the complete secularism of our age. Not even a
broken myth, demythologized and explained in terms of
Jung and depth psychology will suffice. Our generation has
outgrown not only the myth but also any possible interpretation of the myth. Thus modern society is not only secular and
nonmythological, but monochromatic and unidimensional — it
sees life and reality all on one level, the material. The appeals
of Tillich and others of his generation to the " depths of life "
invoked by the " meaning " of the old myths are expressions of
beliefs and sensibilities that we no longer share.

Ultimately, in such a situation as ours, only the most radical
attempts to redefine and reestablish the sense of the sacred have
any chance of success. Altizer, Hamilton, and van Buren, along
with a great many other younger theologians who share their
radical vision, are struggling to reunite modern man's mind and
spirit, his historic self-consciousness, with its scientific view
of the world and his capacity for self-sacrifice and self-transcendence. The older neo-orthodoxy of Barth only drove the
wedge deeper and split man's mind and spirit farther apart,
and the radicals therefore have reacted against the neo-orthodox doctrine of the sovereignty of God because they feared its
disintegrating effect on man's character. We may note that the
whole aim of Tillich's theology was to transcend reason and to
unite man's mind and spirit with the Divine, which he defined
as the abyss of meaning and being, and that the radicals have
not given Tillich's theological judgments the seriousness they
deserve. But considering the situation in which we live, the
open-minded man can only support the tentative experiments
of the radical theologians, since the repetition of the answers
of the past will not fit the new questions raised by the problems of today.

Chapter VI
The Future of Theology

WE HAVE COME a long way in our discussion of "the contrapuntal tradition" which has existed side by side with the "orthodox tradition" in Western culture and religion throughout its twenty-five-hundred-year history. In Chapter V, we arrived at our own day, the era of the recognition of "the death of God," and introduced the recent radical theological movement of Altizer, Hamilton, and van Buren. Now it is time to investigate the elements in our cultural tradition which have provoked the rise of this most radical of movements. We shall carry through this investigation by use of some of the literary documents produced in our times and by reference to the prevailing social movements that have shaped our era. We shall find that the dramatists and novelists of the past three decades have monitored the essential element in the "God is dead" culture, our common sense of the loss of the conviction of God's transcendence, and the consequent loss of the hope for human self-transcendence. We shall also find that the increasing social sensitivity of the American people, as seen in the civil rights movement and in the reaction against war, is part of the complex of influences that have brought about a serious hearing for "the death of God" movement.

The Sense of Our Loss of the Dimension of Transcendence

For a multitude of reasons, which we hope to illustrate briefly here, there is a widespread feeling today that we no longer sense the dimension of transcendence in life in ways that men of the past apparently sensed it. Men today know, with a tinge of regret, that the stars in the sky do not move them to feelings of reverence and awe as they did the ancients — or even men of a few hundred years ago. Kant, surely no primitive personality, spoke of the sense of reverence produced in him by the sight of the starry sky, but this experience is apparently rare in our day. William Hamilton has written of an experience with his son that illustrates this phenomenon:

The other night I was out in the back-yard with one of my children who had to identify some constellation for his science homework. . . . May son is a full citizen of the modern world, and said to me, after he had located the required constellations, "Which are the ones we put up there, Dad?" . . . He had become a technological man, and this means something religiously.[1]

This phenomenon of understanding the world scientifically (even if it is only pseudoscientifically) is one of the characteristic elements in our daily life. It is not part of our mental equipment today to attribute phenomena like stars or earthquakes directly to God, as was the case centuries ago. Even the terrible power seen in natural disasters such as hurricanes no longer gives us a sense of the transcendent power of God. Hamilton has remarked that modern men no longer need God as a meeter of needs or a solver of problems. For assistance in need or in disaster, men turn to the human community and to the available resources of science. Hamilton suggests that men today need to turn to the human community for comfort under adversity also, instead of to " God."[2]

There is much more involved in the modern loss of a transcendent sense than this pragmatic reliance upon human resources. For centuries men have felt that "God helps those who help themselves." Why should our age differ from previous ages in the sense of dropping the reference to God — and with it reference to a transcendent dimension of life? For an answer to this question we now turn to the analysis of twentieth-century American culture given by one of America's foremost dramatists, Eugene O'Neill. Through his works we shall see that the loss of the sense of transcendence, the loss of majesty, of nobility, of victory, is shared by our whole cultural community.

Eugene O'Neill (1888–1953) was, by common consent, America's greatest playwright.[3] There is little need for us to discuss O'Neill's personal life, since his philosophy of skepticism and frustration, as well as his constant search for a lost God, is adequately recorded in his plays. O'Neill was a pessimistic man who suffered from tuberculosis, and was unhappily married and divorced several times. O'Neill has intimated that he was always "a little in love with death,"[4] and this feeling comes to expression in many of his plays.

The three great bases on which O'Neill developed the themes of his plays, besides his own tragic life experiences, are the ancient Greek tragedies of Aeschylus, Sophocles, and Euripides, the psychoanalysis of Sigmund Freud, and the dramas of August Strindberg.[5] O'Neill's plays include *Beyond the Horizon* (1920); *The Emperor Jones* (1920); *Anna Christie* (1921); *The Hairy Ape* (1922); *Desire Under the Elms* (1924); *The Great God Brown* (1926); *Strange Interlude* (1928); *Lazarus Laughed* (1927); *Dynamo* (1929); *Mourning Becomes Electra* (1931); *Ah, Wilderness!* (1933); *Days Without End* (1934); *The Iceman Cometh* (written, 1939, produced 1946); and *Long Day's Journey Into Night* (1955).

The physical production of O'Neill's plays reveals his dependence upon the Greek dramatists. In *The Great God Brown,* O'Neill made use of the ancient dramatic masks, and in *Strange Interlude* and *Mourning Becomes Electra,* O'Neill spiritualized the mask and substituted a stony set of face that gives the appearance of a mask. O'Neill produced his greatest work, *Mourning Becomes Electra*, by mixing Freudian psychology and the ancient theme of family murder. In this play, in its day the longest ever presented on an American stage, O'Neill mixed Greek fate and Freud's Oedipus and Electra complexes and produced a semitragedy of great power. As O'Neill rounded out the play by adding the Oedipus myth to the original Electra myth, we see that he was more indebted to Freud than to Sophocles. O'Neill was also influenced by the culture-shaking events of his lifetime. The wasteland atmosphere of the post-World War I period and the tragedy of the depression affected him. O'Neill quite probably was not influenced by European existentialism, but the same kind of events that brought about the rise of existentialism shaped his dramatic vision.

O'Neill's work falls into four periods:

The first period, 1916–1928, includes the naturalistic and expressionistic plays beginning with *The S.S. Glencairn Series* to *Strange Interlude*. These plays, long and depressing, made use of the Greek mask.

The second period, 1928–1931, includes O'Neill's modern revival of classic Greek tragedy. These plays, exemplified by *Mourning Becomes Electra*, show a blend of Greek tragedy and Freudian thought.

The third period, 1932–1934, includes only one play, *Days Without End*, which is the most world-affirming and religious of all O'Neill's work. The chief character of this play, John Loving, is a split personality, and the two parts of his personality are played by two actors, dressed identically, who always appear together on the stage. At the end of the play, the character's personality is integrated by faith in the " Son of Man."

O'Neill spent the next twelve years in retirement.

The fourth and last period, 1939–1953, is one in which O'Neill reverted to complete pessimism. *The Iceman Cometh*, written in 1939, but not produced until 1946, is one of the most nihilistic plays every produced. O'Neill wrote of the bums and drifters he met in his travels as a youth. The "hero" is a bum named Hickey who, we are led to believe, has committed the unforgivable sin and cannot repent of it. O'Neill explores the web of lies and illusions which keep the bums alive, and the point of the play seems to be that no man can live without his illusions — even when he knows that they are false.

O'Neill was an atheist. To him, God — the God of the traditional Christian church — was dead. He was truly the "Apostle of Skepticism," yet he saw unfaith as man's greatest curse. However, he was too skeptical to believe fully in either the "logical positivism" of modern scientific thought or in the dogma of Christianity. He was not content to be a mere "naysayer," however, and he actually tried to manufacture a new god for modern life, but of course, he failed. With Jean-Paul Sartre, O'Neill could genuinely say:

God is dead, but man has not for all that become atheistic. . . . Hegel tried to replace him with a system. . . . Comte, by a religion of humanity, [both] systems failed. . . . God is silent and that I cannot deny — [but] everything in myself calls for God and that I cannot forget.[6]

Thus O'Neill proposed to find himself a new god, one that would "fill the bill" and be more personal than the "absolute" of idealistic philosophy, and more "intellectually acceptable" than the God of the traditional church.

Robert Warnock has written:

For O'Neill the revolution wrought by physical science and psychoanalysis has not destroyed the realities of older periods of man's spiritual life, but given him a new understanding of their meaning. To the interpretation of these spiritual realities he has brought not simply the soul-baring realism if Strindberg and Freud, but also the cumulated tradition of centuries of inquiry. He believes that facing the truth about the nature of man, however unpleasant, must precede any final security.

Like Socrates he must know before he can find contentment and rest. Like Dante he must go through the Inferno of horror and disillusionment to reach the truth and the eventual peace of the spirit.[7]

At the time Warnock wrote, what he says here was true, but, of course, after 1946, and the reversion to nihilism and abject pessimism in *The Iceman Cometh,* it was clearly shown that O'Neill was never to see the stars after ascending from the Inferno as Dante did.

Concerning the play *Dynamo,* O'Neill had this to say:

The play is a symbolical and factual biography of what is happening in a large section of the American (and not only the American) soul right now It is really the first play of a trilogy that will dig at the roots of the sickness as I feel it — the death of an old God and the failure of science and materialism to give any satisfying new one for the surviving primitive religious instinct to find a meaning for life in, and to comfort its fears of death with. . . . The other two plays will be " Without Ending of Days " and " It Cannot be Mad." [8]

But nothing ever came of this grand scheme. He did write *Days Without End,* and it was a religious play. It seemed for a time that he had come to faith at last; but he never wrote, or at least never published or produced *It Cannot Be Mad.* The question remains, What happened to O'Neill after he wrote *Days Without End?* Perhaps O'Neill came to believe the lines he wrote as a young newspaper reporter in 1912:

When truth and love and God are dead. It is time, full time to die.[9]

A major element in O'Neill's philosophy is evident, despair. He felt the " sickness unto death " just as Kierkegaard did, but this dread did not lead him to " fear and trembling," to humility before God, as it did for the gloomy Dane. Because of this unrelieved and rebellious despair, O'Neill was much more egocentric that the average man who is merely selfish. O'Neill was obsessed with self-fulfillment (perhaps because of his idolatry of Freud), and he was obsessed with the fear of frustration. These two themes alone run through most of his plays.

O'Neill's basic insight into modern life appears to be that there is no redemption possible. Man is a walking corpse, his soul is dead. This is the message of *The Iceman Cometh,* and it is the note on which O'Neill's life ended. O'Neill was buried, at his own direction, with no funeral service of any kind. He was evidently a complete nihilist at the last. O'Neill differed from the pagan (but religious) Greek dramatists in the spiritual insights he saw in his characters once he had exposed the depths of their souls. O'Neill saw only torment and suffering and no answer to the problems of life; Aeschylus saw torment and suffering which led to repentance and a refining fire which ultimately ended in Orestes' acquittal and restoration. In O'Neill, there is no repentance and restoration; Orin (Orestes) commits suicide and Lavinia (Electra) punishes herself for life. The Greek is spiritual and moral, God is in the play, and he brings restoration and forgiveness. In O'Neill, there is no moral and no God. The maladjustments are permanent, forgiveness is unknown, and there is no salvation.

Arthur Miller (1915–   ) is the author of several dramas that penetrate the American social situation to reveal the problems of our era. Miller's *All My Sons* (1947) portrayed the agony brought about by a small industrialist's sale of defective engines to the Air Corps in World War II. *Death of a Salesman* (1949) is an attempt to present a tragedy with a nonhero. Willy Loman is the picture of a small-time salesman who longed to be rich and popular, but was neither. The play is a keen indictment of the materialistic philosophy underlying American capitalism. Willy Loman is said to have never known who he was, and he is shown never to have even imagined there could be an element of transcendence in life. Willy wanted only money and the good opinion of others that the possession of money would bring. *The Crucible*

(1953) was a play that denounced the religious intolerance that produced the Salem witch trials. Considering the era in which it appeared in America, this play might be understood as an allegory on the Congressional hearings into Communist influence in America conducted during the 1950's by Senator Joseph R. McCarthy. Miller produced two short plays in 1955, *A View from the Bridge* and *A Memory of Two Mondays*. In 1963, Miller presented what critics have called his finest play, *After the Fall*.

The central problem of our culture with which Miller deals in his plays is the problem of communication. Miller shows us characters who are unable to speak to each other about the deepest things in their own minds, either because they are not able to articulate their feelings for themselves or because they are precluded from an awareness of those feelings by the rush for material success in life. Willy Loman is insular, cut off from any depth in his own personality and from genuine conversation with others. Miller shows us modern man in the midst of the trials of everyday family life. This man comes across the footlights as a man with a wrong sense of values. He has no sense of calling, no vocation in life, and hence he lacks any sense of the dimension of transcendence that could give him a goal beyond money. God is not a factor in the life of Miller's characters, yet Miller does not speak of despair as O'Neill did. He calls for a social consciousness in *All My Sons*. Miller also calls for an affirmation of the value of life, as he says in *The Crucible*:

Life, woman, life is God's most precious gift; no principle, however glorious, may justify the taking of it.[10]

This is a noble passage and it shows a drive for integrity that becomes increasingly clear in Miller's latest works. But like O'Neill, Miller is a witness to a culture that lacks a sense of transcendence.

The Rise of Religiosity and the Breakdown of the Religious Dimension in American Life

The period after 1945 to 1955 witnessed a widespread growth of church membership in America, and the rise of the advertising-agency-directed revival movement. The percentage of the population affiliated with the church reached record highs, and evangelistic crusades attracted thousands to their meetings. This series of events, which was concretized by the building of thousands of churches, seems to be in direct opposition to the claim that this is a period that has experienced "the death of God" through a general loss of the sense of transcendence. The conservative or orthodox forces in the church have made much of this period of growth and therefore are angered by critical references to this element of our culture, but most serious observers of the religious scene have agreed that the drive behind the rise in church membership has been that of religiosity or false faith instead of genuine piety. The reasons behind such a judgment are clear, for the major element in the evangelistic messages preached to the people of this era has largely been the appeal to accept God and religion for the good they will do the individual and the nation rather than out of any sense of transcendence over one's mundane concerns. Gabriel Vahanian has ably documented this movement in his book *The Death of God*.[11] Vahanian has observed that the religion of the modern period is actually a religiosity based on the unconscious idea that God is dead. Vahanian's thesis is that the age of mass church membership in America is one that stresses the immanent values of religion rather than the transcendent judgment upon all cultures. He has written that "God dies as soon as he becomes a cultural accessory of a human ideal."[12] Vahanian, tracing the various foibles of the religiosity of mass evangelistic Protestantism, concludes that we are living in a post-Christian era. He declares that our Christianity is post-Christian because it is moralistic, a kind of psychological and emotional welfare-statism. Men are told that they should believe in God because it will keep them from falling prey to drink, keep their children from becoming delinquent, and most of all, will keep America safe from the Communists. Vahanian suggests that the inner sense of the utter emptiness of much Protestant preaching has turned men toward the specter of Communism in order to give some content to their faith. Since there is a lack of transcendence in what they are taught to believe, men who are desperate to believe something turn Christianity into an anti-Communist crusade. It is instructive on this point to recall that during the period of deism, when most of the orthodox ideas of God were dying, men refuse to give up their beliefs in witches and in demons. When men can no longer believe in the transcendent power of goodness, it appears that they substitute belief in the terrible powers of evil.

The period after 1955 to the present has shown a decrease in the growth rate of American religiosity. Each year the number of church members tends to decrease in proportion to the growth of our population. Church officials are finding it more and more difficult to obtain the huge amount of contributions needed to finance their wide-ranging building programs. However, this factor no more proves the loss of the sense of transcendence than the success of Protestant evangelism in the previous period disproved our thesis. The last decade has shown a general tendency among the young, particularly among college students, to drift away from organized religion into an American version of existentialism as their outlook on life. This youthful existentialism contains many noble elements, being far more influenced by Albert Camus than Jean-Paul Sartre. It includes an urgent sense of social consciousness that echoes the beliefs of Camus that we are all responsible for each other. The generation that has come to maturity since 1955 is a generation that keenly feels the injustices that have been historically incorporated within the fabric of American life. This is the generation that has participated in the drive for Negro equality, and has demonstrated against the war in Vietnam. Many of these young people are connected with the church or synagogue, but their real faith seems to be in man and in the potentiality of man to overcome age-old problems of hatred and selfishness.

There is a note of optimism in this generation, an optimism that impels hundreds of young people to demonstrate in Mississippi and face the dangers that this involves out of a belief that they can do something to change a society that has been static for over a century. There is an element of faith in the underlying desire of all mankind for peace in this generation that sends them to teach-ins against war in the belief that if America would stop fighting, everyone else would too. It is a naïve belief, for history does not bear it out; yet it is a noble belief. In a very real sense the racial revolution in America and the disaffection of a significant part of the younger generation from the American role of military guardian of the Western world and its allies, is an evidence of a new sense of transcendence. It is not the sense of the transcendence of the Biblical God or of the philosophical idealism of the nineteenth century — indeed, it is not transcendental at all — but it is a sense of the potentiality of goodness in mankind that is a kind of immanent transcendence in its own right. Since the radical immanence that underlies the younger generation contains the element of judgment and articulates itself as a call for change and reform, it is akin to the contrapuntal tradition that has been the voice of criticism throughout the history of the Western world. It is liberal in the widest sense, and its affinities are with the liberal elements of our society. And since it judges our society and finds it wanting, the immanent transcendence of the student groups is in radical opposition to the conservative, nation-affirming immanence of Protestant religiosity.

However, as positively as we would like to judge the social sensitivity and optimism of the student movements, we must observe that it is a philosophy that utterly lacks a sense of the transcendence of the Divine. It is the finest philosophy we have, but it is a philosophy that has developed under the impact of a culture that is experiencing the absence, if not the death, of God. It should not be surprising to find that all the elements of the radical immanence of the integration and anti-war movements are included in the radical new theology that proclaims the death of God.

The Gospel of Christian Atheism

The most thoroughgoing response to the breakdown of Protestant orthodoxy and the rise of a cultural religion that expressed itself is a religiosity more concerned with the nation than with God is the theology of the left of Thomas J. J. Altizer. In this concluding section we shall examine something of the meaning of the contrapuntal or critical tradition for the religion and culture of our day. One thing seems very clear: the orthodox proclamation of Christianity, and the Western culture based on it, has dissolved into ineffectual fragments in our time. If Christianity is to survive in what is generally recognized as a post-Christian era, Christianity will have to show itself to be far more creative and adventurous than it has been up to this time.

In looking at the theological efforts of the past twenty years, we see encouraging signs that a new creative effort is being made to establish the Christian religion as the spirit of Western culture and to visualize culture as the form or shape of the Christian religion. These signs are the work of Bultmann and Tillich, joined now by the posthumous publication of the penetrating thought of the Jesuit scholar, Pierre Teilhard de Chardin. We shall develop a little later the significance of Teilhard for the future of Western religion, as he represents — along with Tillich — a possible synthesis of " orthdox " insights with the most radical insights of our technological era. The last decade has also brought forward the theology of the left,

which proclaims the necessity of accepting the death of the
God of the Bible and Christian theology as a redemptive event.
This movement, as important as it is, apparently lacks the balance of the system developed by Tillich and Teilhard. However, the radical theology will remain an important element
in religious thinking for a long time to come, as it is, in many
senses, merely the exaggeration of the elements in the contrapuntal tradition that were provoked by the failure of Western
orthodoxy.

The Future of Theology from the Standpoint of the Left Wing

For Thomas Altizer the theology of today and tomorrow
must be a free theology. It must be the proclamation of a
theologian who does not speak in defense of the church, even
if he speaks as a critic in the vanguard of a progressive world
view. The new theology must speak of the good news of Christianity which includes the message of the death of God. It
means that God has died in order to free man and that Jesus,
who was radically loving and helpful, has been resurrected —
in a manner of speaking — in the human race. Altizer says that
the first duty of the theologian today is loyalty to this Christ
who is present in the totality of human experience. Therefore,
the radical theologian sees as his task the proclamation of the
example of the apocalyptic Jesus of the Gospels, in whose message and example God completely revealed himself and thus
willed to die in order to bring about man's salvation in the
freedom of Jesus. In this way Altizer offers our time the possibility of a recovery of the sense of transcendence. In faithful-
ness to the love and self-sacrifice of the radical Jesus, there is
the possibility of man individually and as a race achieving
human self-transcendence. This human self-transcendence Altizer calls "Man-Godhood," basing his thought in part upon
the "essential God-manhood" of Tillich's Christology.

William Hamilton offers a variant conception of the role of
Jesus in left-wing theology, Jesus as *Vorbild* or model, which

he sometimes describes as Jesus as *Locus* or the place for the Christian to be. As Hamilton sees the chief barrier to belief in God in the problem of suffering, it is necessary in his view to see Jesus as the companion of the civil rights worker in the struggle for human rights and as the war protestor in the struggle against the destructiveness of war. Hamilton would give great weight to the decades of war and persecution which the twentieth century has endured as an element in the decline of belief in God. He has recently written:

If for you there is nothing special about the 20th Century's experience of suffering, then this line of argument will not persuade. This has always been unmerited suffering in the world, and it has always been a problem for the heart and the head to hold to the reality of suffering and to the goodness and power of God at the same time. It has always been hard, I am saying, and now it is impossible; for the terrible burden of suffering our time has witnessed can be ascribed to God only by turning him into a monster.[18]

The problem of suffering identified by Hamilton and the problem of the loss of human morale, which grows out of the lack of the experience of self-transcendence, identified by O'Neill in his plays, are closely related. Men have always suffered, and have even courted suffering, as in the case of the early Christian martyrs and in the crusades, but the experience of self-transcendence gave meaning to their suffering. Similarly, the suffering of the revolutionists in the American Revolutionary War was given meaning and value by the ideal which stretched before them. However, there is no sense of transcendence in the tens of millions of deaths brought about by the World Wars and the smaller wars of the twentieth century. What could be morally elevating about struggles which destroyed the fabric of the twenty-five-hundred-year-old culture, and destroyed civilian populations as well as soldiers. In this brutality, epitomized by the concentration camps, modern man saw through the facade of his philosophies and cultural

religions. It was, after all, Christian nations that produced
these horrors. Man lost his sense of being part of a culture that
was capped with the benevolent guidance of God. All sensitive spirits had to revolt against the belief that this suffering
was somehow good. Now there could be only one goal, a goal
clearly subscribed to by Altizer and Hamilton, and by the spiritually sensitive activists of the civil rights movement and the
protest against war, the elimination of human suffering and the
strengthening of human good will. In the words of Camus to a
group of Catholic monks:

And, as for me, I feel rather as Augustine did before becoming
a Christian when he said: "I tried to find the source of evil
and I got nowhere." But it is also true that I, and a few others,
know what must be done, if not to reduce evil, at least not to
add to it. Perhaps we cannot prevent this world from being a
world in which children are tortured. But we can reduce the
number of tortured children. And if you don't help us, who
else in the world can help us do this?[14]

Without hesitation, the Christian of today must say to
Camus, "Yes, we will help to fight evil and overcome suffering."
The radical theologians have said yes too. This is their
strength, that they place the locus of the recovery of the sense
of transcendence (which Altizer calls the experience of the
sacred) in the radically immanent everyday life of man. If man
is to recover a sense of meaning for his life that is more than
the satisfaction of physical wants or the accumulation of material possessions, then — in order to meet the first requirement
of being a man — he must find his sense of identity in his capacity to identify the negative elements in life and find his maturity and success in the struggle against them. Such an identification of oneself with the positively human figures of history,
such as Jesus, St. Francis, Schweitzer, and others, is the beginning of a sense of self-identity that transcends the identification
of oneself as a machine tender, a Democrat, a white man or
Negro, etc., and makes one sense his participation in the on-

going process of life. Such a man is a radical Christian who involves himself in the struggle for social justice, in the efforts
to overcome disease and mental illness, and, above all, in the
struggle for peace among men. To achieve such a sense of
identity, with a consequent sense of transcendence, indeed
involves a kind of death. It must experience a death to every
partial identification of the self with a creed, class, race, or nation. It must be a death of one's solidarity with the human institution of the church, and a death of one's acceptance or
tolerance of mythological forms of religious expression.

This is the challenge of the radical theology, that men part
with the ideals and philosophic abstractions that have been
identified as " God " along with all those beautiful and artistic
myths and symbols that pointed to some cosmic life and purpose apart from man that works its will either with man or by
man, apart from human achievement. The radical theology
locates the transcendent of the Divine within the immanence
of the human, and challenges man to live up to his profession
of reverence for those kinds of conduct he has historically
called the attributes of God. This is a clear call, akin to the
challenge of Feuerbach in the last century, and any future
theology that our post-Christian era may produce must take
its challenge seriously. The radical theologian has not given all
the answers to the problems of man, but he has done a more
important thing: he has laid out the route that theology must
follow from this point.

Any future theology must respond to the radicals as the
bearers of the prophetic spirit of Protestantism. It must see that
Jesus is indeed a symbol of human possibility, the possibility of
human goodness and cooperation overcoming suffering and
warfare. It must accept the identification of the integrative and
socializing functions of Western culture as a mark of the presence of that Jesus who commanded men to love one another.
Future theology must overcome its initial negative evaluation
of the radical movement, if theology is not to become a reac-

tionary element in a world that is moving too fast ever to return to any former position, no matter how noble. Theology must see the radical movement — in religion and politics — as religious loyalty cutting into religion and political loyalty cutting into politics. Future theology must not call the radical movement " atheism " in any other sense than it has identified itself, as " Christian Atheism." True atheism, all must agree, is marked by an absence of that ultimate concern which makes man critical of the " object " of his faith, and true political treason is marked by an absence of that reverence for principle which makes one rebel against compromises of the ideals that underlie the state and people from which we came and to which we belong.

The death and the resurrection of the radical theology is not an agnostic " as if "; it is real in the ultimate sense. It is not easy to experience, although it may be simple to explain. The acceptance of the elements that are positive and prophetic in this movement will not be easy, but many will accept them. Such acceptance will come only after struggle, for the radical theology apparently goes against the grain of everything that we thought we believed and for which we may have worked, sacrificed, and fought. The Romans who saw in the message about Jesus only a subversive threat to the state and an atheistic stance against the gods, but who in increasing numbers came to embrace Christianity underwent this kind of struggle. The acceptance of the inner meaning of the message of " the death of God " and the acceptance of the secular, the radically immanent as the sole locus of the transcendent, will be an experience of death. But if human hope has any basis in the concrete events of the world processes, man may find in the depths of the profane a historical kind of resurrection in the development of love and cooperation among men that will cancel out the horrors of history and free man from the inner alienation within himself and the outward alienation of self from self that makes up the tragic element in the human fabric of history.

Pierre Teilhard de Chardin: An Indicator of the Future
Pilgrimage That Must Be Followed by Western Theology

Pierre Teilhard de Chardin (1881–1955) was a distinguished paleontologist and French Jesuit scholar who combined a sensitive religious life with an acute scientific understanding of the world. Teilhard's works were not published during his lifetime because of the censorship imposed on him by the Roman Catholic hierarchy which feared the radicalness of his views. Since 1955, there has been a steady stream of books by and about Teilhard in French and in English, which has made his thought available to the world. Teilhard's first published work is a radically different approach to the evolution of life, *The Phenomenon of Man.*[15] In it he evolved a theory of the development of matter (" pre-life ") into life, and of the turning in upon itself (" reflexion ") of life that produced thought — mankind itself. Teilhard moved on through his scientific material to speak of a future " personalizing " of the universe in which the cosmos is seen as evolving to " the Omega point " where it becomes united with God. Thus Teilhard saw evolution as driving toward the kind of Christ mysticism and ultimate unity with God that is spoken of in Ephesians anl Colossians:

For he [God] has made known to us in all wisdom and insight the mystery of his will, according to his purpose which he set forth in Christ as a plan for the fulness of time, to unite all things in him, things in heaven and things on earth. (Eph. 1:9-10.)

Other works by Teilhard include *The Divine Milieu,*[16] which is a study in the radical immanence of spirituality. Uniquely, Teilhard subtitled this work " An Essay on the Interior Life," and dedicated it " For those who love the world." Teilhard wrote that the Christian problem is the sanctification of action, and suggested that men should attempt to spiritualize both their activities and their passivities, which would lead to the final solution of humanity's age-old problems — the completion of the world through human activity " in Christ Jesus." Teilhard suggested that such a motivation and activity would bring about "the divine milieu" in which man's struggle against evil would be won by God's help. In this higher order of life every individual would find fulfillment and the human race would realize the progress that can only come when men consider themselves part of a single social and spiritual community. Another of Teilhard's works is *The Future of Man*.[17] This is a collection of essays that point out his belief that human faith in the evolution of life and Christian faith in the salvation of life can be harmonized in a view that sees humanity as evolving into a living collectivity of fellowship that will ultimately end in the unity of God and man in "Christogenesis."

In *Pierre Teilhard de Chardin: His Life and Spirit*, Nicolas Corte (a pseudonym used by a Catholic scholar) reports that Teilhard wrote as early as 1936:

Now every human action raises the problem of God, and that problem can't be attacked except by the total effort of human research and experience. Not only does God give an eternal value to the effort of man, but His revelation is a response to the totality of human effort.[18]

For Teilhard, every human action not only raises the problem of God but has its part in the life of God. In a very real sense, he is speaking of the same kind of future for Christianity that Altizer and Hamilton are. In *The Divine Milieu*, Teilhard writes of man today waiting "in expectation of the parousia," [19] that is, waiting for the coming of the evolution of the world toward union with God. In this epilogue, he speaks frankly of the human situation, saying that while Christians may claim to look for the coming of the Kingdom of God, in reality, "we no longer expect anything." [20] He suggests that we might recapture this transcendental expectation if we embodied it in a "huge and totally human hope." [21] Teilhard meant, of course, that modern man should see the world as the creation of God which is doubly infused by divine power because of the incarnation of Christ. He believed that by loving the earth — and especially loving man, who is the crown of the evolution of the earth — one loved God and advanced the day that would reveal his glory. He believed that all the forces that tended to draw men together — scientific studies, modern means of communication, the growth of liberal social democracy, and the increasing dependence of man upon man that is resolving both Western and Eastern society into socialistically based communities — all contributed to the growth of the "noosphere" or corporate humanity, in which all men are to become part of one living organism that covers the face of the world. Teilhard developed these thoughts at length in his essays "Turmoil or Genesis?" and "The Directions and Conditions of the Future" in *The Future of Man*.[22]

In a very real sense, what Teilhard foresaw is a future in which man is to grow closer to man. Man is to react positively to the problem of suffering and work and fight to overcome all those conditions which keep men from coming to their full development or that murder them in the course of senseless war. In this struggle toward human community, Teilhard welcomed the help of all men. He was the friend of non-Christians, Christians, and men of other faiths; and he believed that the ultimate Parousia would be the salvation of all mankind. Teilhard believed that all those things which divide man from man must be "died to," and that we should look to Jesus for the example of charity that will make the ultimate community of man a reality. Of course, Jesus is, for Teilhard, not only human possibility, as he is for the radical theologians; he is also the cosmic Christ. But in the last analysis, what Teilhard calls for is the kind of human endeavor that imitates the openness to others and affirmation of life that the radicals proclaim about Jesus.

In his writings, Teilhard reveals himself to be one of the great human figures who loved mankind while loving God as well. Without doubt, he was the faithful Catholic he professed to be, and so he believed much more than any of the radical theologians can believe, and perhaps more than anyone now living can believe. But Teilhard, like Tillich, believed in the historically conditioned message of Christianity in his own unique way. In Teilhard's case, surely the concept of universal evolution has replaced the mythological doctrine of the salvation brought by Christ. For him, no less than for the radicals, the God he worshiped was the eschatological God of the ultimate consummation — the future God, the cosmic Christ — who would arise out of the eternally evolving human race — the goal and the motivation of every sensitive man who seeks to socialize and personalize a world of matter into a dimension of spirit. Teilhard reveals something of this hope for the coming of a true divinity in the universe in these words:

So that the greatest event in the history of the Earth, now taking place, may be the gradual discovery, by those with eyes to see, not merely of Something but of *Someone* at the peak created by the convergence of the evolving Universe upon itself.[23]

If there is to be a future theology that will speak of the Divine in terms that do not simply hallow the selfish position of one class or race or nation but that point beyond itself to the ultimate and transcending as the source and goal of the human adventure, it will have to come into being through the study of the radical thinkers of our time. The problem of God, which some have called the problem of modern theology, will be found to be the problem of fully expressing the human spirit. In the search for understanding of that mysterious milieu out of which the human spirit has arisen and toward which it evolves, Teilhard de Chardin will be the Dante who will guide us from the purgatory of the present to the reality of faith in the transcendent future. The spirit of any viable future Christian philosophy or theology lies in a creative blend of the mysticism and social sensitivity of Teilhard, Altizer, and Hamilton. It will be a theology that sees the transcendent within this world, for it will be based on a philosophy that recognizes no other world.

The time to begin the theology of the future is now. Only the most radical attempts to recover the sense of the sacred and the experience of self-transcendence have any chance of success. A repetition of the Christian positions of the past will do nothing but hinder the possibility that the God of the future might be at least partially known in our time.

Notes

I. The Contrapuntal Tradition in the West

1. Ludwig Feuerbach, *The Essence of Christianity*, tr. by George Eliot (Harper Torchbooks, 1957), from the " Introduction," by Karl Barth, p. xi.

2. *Ibid.*, p. xiii.

3. Friedrich Nietzsche, *The Philosophy of Nietzsche* (The Modern Library, Inc., 1954). Quote from *Thus Spake Zarathustra*, Ch. 73, 2, p. 320.

4. *Ibid.*, p. 321.

5. *Ibid.*, p. 96.

6. Nietzsche's deep involvement with Christianity is well documented in Karl Jaspers, *Nietzsche and Christianity* (Henry Regnery Company, 1961).

7. Thomas J. J. Altizer and William Hamilton, *Radical Theology and the Death of God* (The Bobbs-Merrill Company, Inc., 1966).

8. *Ibid.*, pp. ix–x.

9. *Ibid.*, p. x.

10. Harvey Cox, *The Secular City* (The Macmillan Company, 1965).

11. Paul Tillich, *The Courage to Be* (Yale University Press, 1952).

12. Paul Tillich, *The Dynamics of Faith* (Harper Torchbooks, 1957), pp. 41–43.

13. William Hamilton, *The New Essence of Christianity* (Association Press, 1961).

14. Dietrich Bonhoeffer, *Prisoner for God,* ed. by Eberhard Bethge, tr. by Reginald H. Fuller (American title of *Letters and Papers from Prison*) (The Macmillan Company, 1953).

15. *Ibid.,* p. 124.

16. *Ibid.*

17. *Ibid.,* p. 123.

18. *Ibid.,* pp. 123–124.

19. *Ibid.,* pp. 163–164.

20. Altizer and Hamilton, *op. cit.,* pp. x–xi.

21. *Ibid.,* p. x.

22. *Ibid.*

23. Nietzsche, *op. cit.,* p. 96.

24. Martin Luther is credited with the phrase " God Himself has died," by Hegel in *Phenomenology of the Mind,* tr. by J. B. Baillie (The Macmillan Company, 1919), p. 762. This phrase apparently occurs in one of Luther's Lenten chorales, but this writer has not been able to locate it. See also J. N. Findlay, *Hegel: A Re-examination* (Collier Books, 1962), p. 142. According to C. R. McCormack, *Frontiers,* Vol. XVII, No. 8 (April, 1966), pp. 9–10, the phrase " God is dead " is taken from a hymn written in 1641 by a Lutheran, Johann Rist.

25. See the essays " Word and History " and " The Sacred and the Profane," Altizer and Hamilton, *op. cit.,* pp. 121 ff.; 140 ff.

26. Nietzsche, *op. cit.,* p. 153.

27. Walter Lowrie, *Kierkegaord* (two vols., Harper Torchbooks, 1962), Vol. I, p. 3.

28. From *The Journal of Kierkegaard,* p. 317, quoted in Lowrie, *op. cit.,* Vol. I, p. 164.

29. Søren Kierkegaard, *The Philosophical Fragments* (Princeton University Press, 1936).

30. Søren Kierkegaard, *Concluding Unscientific Postscript to the Philosophical Fragments* (Princeton University Press, 1941).

31. Lowrie, *op. cit.,* Vol. II, p. 317.

32. *Ibid.,* p. 489.

33. *Ibid.,* p. 536.

34. *Ibid.,* p. 541.

35. *Ibid.*

36. Karl Marx and Friedrich Engels, *The Communist Manifesto,* ed. by Samuel H. Beer (Appleton-Century-Crofts, Inc., 1955).

37. *Ibid.*, p. 9.

38. W. T. Jones, *A History of Western Philosophy*, Vol. II (Harcourt, Brace and World, Inc., 1952), p. 916.

39. See various books by Marx, e.g., *Das Kapital*, ed. by F. Engels (Gateway ed., Henry Regnery Company, 1965). See also books about Marx: *The God That Failed*, ed. by Richard Crossman (Harper & Brothers, 1950); Robert Nigel Carew Hunt, *Marxism, Past and Present* (The Macmillan Company, 1955); Martin D'Arcy, *Communism and Christianity* (Penguin Books, Inc., 1956); *The Profile of Communism*, ed. by Moster Decter (Collier Books, 1961); George Lichtheim, *Marxism: An Historical and Critical Study* (Frederick A. Praeger Inc., Publishers, 1962); Alfred G. Meyer, *Communism* (2d ed., Random House, Inc., 1962); and *Essential Works of Marxism*, ed. by Arthur P. Mendel (Bantam Books, Inc., 1965).

40. See *The Basic Writings of Sigmund Freud*, tr. and ed. by A. A. Brill (The Modern Library, Inc., 1938), p. 4, and Ernest Jones, *Sigmund Freud* (Basic Books, Inc., 1955), Vol. III, p. 376.

41. Freud, "Totem and Taboo," Brill, *op. cit.*, pp. 807 ff., esp. pp. 903 ff. and 915 ff.

42. *Ibid.*, pp. 915–916.

43. *Ibid.*, p. 916.

44. Julian Huxley, *Religion Without Revelation* (Mentor Books, 1957).

45. Alfred North Whitehead, *Process and Reality* (Harper Torchbooks, 1960), and *Science and the Modern World* (Mentor Books, 1964, 13th printing). Whitehead's dates are 1861–1947.

II. Critical Scholarship and Rationalistic Orthodoxy

1. See, on this whole topic, the classic study by Andrew Dickson White, *A History of the Warfare of Science with Theology in Christendom* (The Macmillan Company, Free Press paperback, 1965; first published in 1896).

2. Nietzsche, *op. cit.*, pp. 951 ff.

3. Immanuel Kant, *Religion Within the Limits of Reason Alone*, tr. by T. M. Greene and H. H. Hudson (Harper Torchbooks, 1960), p. 158.

4. Immanuel Kant, *Critique of Pure Reason*, ed. and tr. by N. K. Smith (St. Martin's Press, 1965).

5. Immanuel Kant, *Critique of Practical Reason*, tr. by L. W. Beck (Library of Liberal Arts, The Bobbs-Merrill Company, Inc., 1956), p. 72.

6. *Ibid.*

7. Lewis White Beck, *Commentary on Kant's Critique of Practical Reason* (The University of Chicago Press, 1960), p. 255.

8. Anselm, *Proslogium*, Ch. II, in *St. Anselm: Basic Writings,* tr. by S. N. Deane (The Open Court Publishing Company, 1962), p. 7.

9. Georg W. F. Hegel, *Lectures on the History of Philosophy,* Vol. III, tr. by E. S. Haldane and F. H. Simson (London, 1896), p. 62.

10. Tillich's system has been greatly influenced by Schleiermacher's theology. See *Systematic Theology,* Vol. II (The University of Chicago Press, 1957), pp. 14, 150.

11. Friedrich Schleiermacher, *On Religion,* tr. by John Oman (Harper Torchbooks, 1958).

12. *Ibid.,* p. 35.

13. *Ibid.,* p. 36.

14. *Ibid.*

15. Friedrich Schleiermacher, *The Christian Faith,* two vols., ed. by H. R. Mackintosh and J. S. Stewart (E. T. of the 2d German ed., Harper Torchbooks, 1963).

16. *Ibid.,* Vol. I, " The Conception of the Church," par. 3, pp. 5 ff.

17. *Ibid.,* p. 8.

18. *Ibid.,* par. 4, p. 12.

19. *Ibid.,* p. 15.

20. *Ibid.,* pp. 15–16.

21. *Ibid.,* p. 16.

22. Schleiermacher, *On Religion.*

23. *Ibid.,* p. 94.

24. Schleiermacher, *The Christian Faith,* Vol. I, par. 53, p. 206.

25. *Ibid.,* p. 17.

26. *Ibid.,* pp. 17–18.

27. *Ibid.,* p. 18.

28. The beginning of the careers of the great Protestant " Synthesizers," which will be discussed in Chapter III.

29. Albert Schweitzer, *The Quest of the Historical Jesus* (London: A. & C. Black, 1910).

30. Martin Kähler, *The So-called Historical Jesus and the Historic Christ,* tr. by Carl Braaten (Fortress Press, 1964). See also James M. Robinson, *The New Quest for the Historical Jesus* (Alec R. Allenson, Inc., 1959).

31. The Jewish orthodox tradition is seen at work in the case of the pious Jewish philosopher, Baruch Spinoza, whose *Tractatus Theologico-Politicus* was condemned by the synagogue as well as the Christian churches.

32. White, *op. cit.,* pp. 466 ff.

33. Edwin Hatch, *The Influence of Greek Ideas on Christianity* (Harper Torchbooks, 1961).

34. See Mircea Eliade, *Cosmos and History: The Myth of the Eternal Return* (Harper Torchbooks, 1959); also, *The Sacred and the Profane* (Harper Torchbooks, 1961).

35. Evidence of the growing influence of the "history of religions" upon theology can be seen in the interest of Paul Tillich in the work of Mircea Eliade during the last period of Tillich's life. Tillich has recorded his views of the place of the "history of religions" in theology in *The Future of Religions* (Harper & Row, Publishers, Inc., 1966). This writer took part in the two years of study and seminars on the interaction of theology and the "history of religions" held by Tillich and Eliade at the University of Chicago, 1963–1965.

36. *Encyclopædia Britannica,* Vol. 7, pp. 83–84.

37. *Encyclopædia Britannica,* Vol. 20, pp. 132–133.

38. *Ibid.,* p. 132.

39. White, *op. cit.,* pp. 189 ff. Gladstone's essay was the "Dawn of Creation and Worship," in *The Nineteenth Century* (November, 1885).

40. Albert Schweitzer, *The Quest of the Historical Jesus: A Critical Study from Reimarus to Wrede,* tr. by W. Montgomery (The Macmillan Company, 1926; first E. T., 1910; J. C. B. Mohr, Tübingen, 1906).

III.   Radical Scholarship and Protestant Piety

1. Charles Harvey Arnold, "Against the Furious Men," *Frontiers*, Vol. XVII, No. 5 (Jan., 1966), p. 8.

2. For a complete survey of the theology of this period, see John Macquarrie, *Twentieth Century Religious Thought: The Frontiers of Philosophy and Theology, 1900–1960* (Harper & Row, Publishers, Inc., 1963), pp. 23–94.

3. Wilhelm Herrmann, *Systematic Theology*, tr. by N. Micklem and K. A. Sanders (The Macmillan Company, 1927).

4. Wilhelm Herrmann, *The Communion of the Christian with God*, tr. by J. S. Stanyon (London: 1895).

5. Herrmann, *Systematic Theology*, p. 40.

6. Schweitzer, *The Quest of the Historical Jesus*, p. 399.

7. Adolf Deissmann, *Paul: A Study in Social and Religious History* (Harper Torchbooks, 1957), 1st ed., 1912.

8. *The Christian Century*, September 7, 1955.

9. Schweitzer, *The Mysticism of Paul the Apostle*, tr. by W. Montgomery (Henry Holt & Company, 1931), p. 3.

10. For more discussion of this point, see John C. Cooper, "Humanitarian in Africa," *Resource*, Vol. 6, No. 9 (June, 1965), pp. 6–9.

11. For a longer introduction to the life and work of Bultmann, see John C. Cooper, "Interpreter of Christianity to the Modern Age," *Resource*, Vol. 8, No. 1 (October, 1966), pp. 16–19.

12. J. Schoneberg Setzer, "The Cosmology of Rudolf Bultmann," *The Lutheran Quarterly*, Vol. XV, No. 2 (May, 1963), p. 158.

13. Hendrik Kraemer, *The Communication of the Christian Faith* (The Westminster Press, 1956).

14. For an introduction to Barth, see John C. Cooper, "Theologian of the Word of God," *Resource*, Vol. 7, No. 1 (Oct., 1965), pp. 2–5.

15. The information contained in this discussion of Bultmann is derived from the following works: (*a*) Hans W. Bartsch (ed.), *Kerygma and Myth* (Harper Torchbooks, 1961); (*b*) Bultmann, *The Theology of the New Testament*, Vol. I (Charles Scribner's Sons, 1951); (*c*) James M. Robinson, *The Bultmann School of Biblical Interpretation: New Directions?* (Harper & Row, Publishers,

Inc., 1965); (*d*) Bultmann, *Translating Theology Into the Modern Age* (Harper & Row, Publishers, Inc., 1965); (*e*) James M. Robinson and John B. Cobb, Jr. (eds.), *The New Hermeneutic*, Vol. II, *New Frontiers in Theology* (Harper & Row, Publishers, Inc., 1964); (*f*) Leonhard Reinisch (ed.), *Theologians of Our Time* (University of Notre Dame Press, 1964).

16. For a discussion of the modern discovery that mythology is a basic element in Christianity, see John C. Cooper, "Mythology and Religion," *Discourse*, Vol. III, No. 2 (Spring, 1964), pp. 129–139.

17. For an interesting discussion of Bultmann's program on a level intelligible to laymen, see Ian Henderson, *Rudolf Bultmann* (John Knox Press, 1966).

18. Jacques Maritain, *Degrees of Knowledge* (Charles Scribner's Sons, 1959), p. 31.

19. Werner Heisenberg, *Physics and Philosophy* (Harper Torchbooks, 1962, first published 1958). See esp. Ch. V.

20. The biographical material in the following discussion of Paul Tillich is taken from Tillich's work, *On the Boundary* (Charles Scribner's Sons, 1966), and first appeared in the format followed here by John C. Cooper in "The Eternal and the Present," *Resource*, Vol. 7, No. 6 (March, 1966), pp. 31–33.

21. For an introduction to Niebuhr's thought, see John C. Cooper, "Spokesman of Christian Concern," *Resource*, Vol. 7, No. 9 (June, 1966), pp. 8–11.

22. Paul Tillich, *The Religious Situation* (Meridian Books, 1956).

23. Charles W. Kegley and Robert W. Bretall (eds.) *The Theology of Paul Tillich* (The Macmillan Company, 1952), p. 7.

24. For a critical assessment of the work of Tillich, done in an appreciative way for laymen, see J. Heywood Thomas, *Paul Tillich* (John Knox Press, 1966). A deeper criticism can be found in Alexander J. McKelway, *The Systematic Theology of Paul Tillich* (John Knox Press, 1964).

25. Tillich's written works fall into three classes. The first class consists of his technical theological works: *Systematic Theology* (Vol. I, 1951; Vol. II, 1957; Vol. III, 1963; The University of Chicago Press). The second class includes Tillich's shorter works writ-

ten for college students and laymen: *The Religious Situation* (Henry Holt & Company, 1932; Meridian Books, 1956); *The Protestant Era* (The University of Chicago Press, 1948); *The Courage to Be* (Yale University Press, 1952); *Love, Power, and Justice* (Oxford University Press, 1954); *Biblical Religion and the Search for Ultimate Reality* (The University of Chicago Press, 1955); *The Dynamics of Faith* (Harper & Brothers, 1957); and *Morality and Beyond* (Harper & Row, Publishers, Inc., 1963). Two of Tillich's works have appeared since his death: *The Future of Religions* (Harper & Row, Publishers, Inc., 1966) and *On the Boundary* (Charles Scribner's Sons, 1966). The third class of books includes Tillich's published sermons: *The Shaking of the Foundations* (Charles Scribner's Sons, 1948); *The New Being* (Charles Scribner's Sons, 1955); and *The Eternal Now* (Charles Scribner's Sons, 1963). Other works by Tillich are: *The Interpretation of History,* tr. by Rasetski and Talmay (Charles Scribner's Sons, 1936); *Theology of Culture* (Oxford University Press, Inc., 1959); and *Christianity and the Encounter of the World Religions* (Columbia University Press, 1963).

26. The information concerning Tillich's theology given herein is excerpted from " The Significance of the Pauline Spirit-Christology for the Doctrine of Spiritual Presence in Paul Tillich," Ph.D. dissertation, the University of Chicago (1966), by John C. Cooper.

27. Tillich, *Systematic Theology*, Vol. II, pp. 107 ff.

28. For a different interpretation of the method of correlation, see B. M. Loomer, " Tillich's Theology of Correlation," *Journal of Religion*, Vol. XXXVI, No. 3 (July, 1956), p. 150.

29. Tillich, *Biblical Religion*, p. 5.

30. " In relation to God, everything is done by God." Tillich, *Systematic Theology*, Vol. III, p. 135. Tillich calls this " the Protestant Principle." It expresses his idea of theonomy.

31. Loomer, *op. cit.*, pp. 150–151.

32. *Ibid.*, pp. 151–152.

33. Tillich, *Systematic Theology*, Vol. II, p. 10.

34. Augustine, *Confessions*, Book I, Ch. I, line 4.

35. This material is based on Tillich, *Systematic Theology*, Vol. I, pp. 168–186.

36. Sydney and Beatrice Rome (eds.), *Philosophical Interroga-*

tions (Holt, Rinehart and Winston, Inc., 1964), pp. 388–389.

37. Tillich, *The Courage to Be*, pp. 182–190.

38. Tillich, *Biblical Religion*, pp. 21–28, 85; *Theology of Culture*, pp. 10–29.

39. Tillich, *Theology of Culture*, pp. 10–29.

40. Additional discussions of Tillich's works that should be consulted for a proper assessment of his theology include: *Christianity and the Existentialists*, ed. by Carl Michalson (Charles Scribner's Sons, 1956); George F. McLean, *Man's Knowledge of God According to Paul Tillich* (Catholic University of America Press, 1958); *Four Existentialist Theologians*, ed. by Will Herberg (Doubleday & Company, Inc., 1958); *The Theology of Paul Tillich*, ed. by C. W. Kegley and Robert W. Bretall (The Macmillan Company, 1961); George H. Tavard, *Paul Tillich and the Christian Message* (Charles Scribner's Sons, 1962); David H. Freeman, *Tillich* (Presbyterian and Reformed Pub. Co., 1962); Kenneth Hamilton, *The System and the Gospel* (The Macmillan Company, 1963); Bernard Martin, *The Existential Theology of Paul Tillich* (Bookman Associates, Inc., 1963); *Paul Tillich in Catholic Thought*, ed. by Thomas A. O'Meara and C. D. Weisser (The Priory Press, 1964); James Luther Adams, *Paul Tillich's Philosophy of Culture, Science, and Religion* (Harper & Row, Publishers, Inc., 1965); and D. Mackenzie Brown, *Ultimate Concern: Tillich in Dialogue* (Harper & Row, Publishers, Inc., 1965).

41. An example of the kind of criticism given to Tillich's attempt to present Christianity in a modern way is the following critique of Carl F. H. Henry, the editor of the conservative Protestant magazine, *Christianity Today*. This quotation is from a letter from Dr. Henry to this writer, dated August 4, 1965: "It seems to me that Tillich shares the same fundamental flaw that runs through the whole movement of anti-intellectual theology. While he does insist that the results of theology and of philosophy must coincide, he nonetheless holds that faith is existential, and denies our possession of cognitive knowledge of transcendent reality, and holds that the affirmations we make about the Unconditioned are symbolic. One who holds that the affirmation or ascription of personality to God is symbolic surely has moved wholly outside the framework of Biblical theology. It seems to me that Tillich marks a deterioration of recent

modern theology from the position of those who assert non-rational, non-objective impersonal theism."

For an appreciative criticism of Tillich that brings his thought into relation with an outstanding psychoanalyst, Erich Fromm, see Guyton B. Hammond, *Man in Estrangement* (Vanderbilt University Press, 1965).

IV. The Divorce of Mind and Spirit

1. Wilfred Owen, "Arms and the Boy," *A Little Treasury of British Poetry,* ed. by Oscar Williams (Charles Scribner's Sons, 1951), p. 704.

2. Erich M. Remarque, *All Quiet on the Western Front* (Lion Books, Inc., 1950), pp. 18–19.

3. *Ibid.,* p. 190.

4. For a discussion of Brunner's work, see John C. Cooper, "Emil Brunner," *Resource,* Vol. 8, No. 4 (Jan., 1967), pp. 2–4.

5. Karl Barth, *Commentary on the Epistle to the Romans,* tr. by E. C. Hoskyns (London: Oxford University Press, 1960).

6. See H. R. Mackintosh, *Types of Modern Theology* (Charles Scribner's Sons, 1937), pp. 263 ff.

7. For information concerning the Russian Revolution and the Civil War which followed it, see Bernard Pares, *Russia* (Mentor Books, 1962); Alan Moorehead, *The Russian Revolution* (Bantam Books, 1959); and Alfred G. Meyer, *Communism* (Random House, Inc., 1962).

8. *Die sozialistische Entscheidung* (Potsdam: Alfred Protte, 1933; suppressed in 1933; reissued in 1948).

9. For a description of the Confessing Church movement, written by those who took part in it, see Hanns Lilje, *The Valley of the Shadow,* tr. by Olive Wyon (Muhlenberg Press, 1950); Dietmar Schmidt, *Pastor Niemöller* (Doubleday & Company, Inc., 1959); Roger Manvell and Heinrich Fraenkel, *The Men Who Tried to Kill Hitler* (Pocket Books, Inc., 1966); Dietrich Bonhoeffer, *Prisoner for God,* ed. by E. Bethge, tr. by Reginald H. Fuller (The Macmillan Company, 1953); Bonhoeffer, *The Cost of Discipleship* (The Macmillan Company, 1963); Bonhoeffer, *Ethics* (The Macmillan Company, 1963); and Bonhoeffer, *No Rusty Swords* (Harper & Row, Publishers, Inc., 1965).

10. Joseph Sittler, *The Ecology of Faith* (Muhlenberg Press, 1961). See also William Hamilton, *The New Essence;* Altizer and Hamilton, *op. cit.*

11. George Santayana, *Interpretation of Poetry and Religion* (Harper Torchbooks, 1957), pp. 85–86.

12. *Ibid.*, p. 86.

13. William Hamilton, *The New Essence,* Ch. 3, pp. 71–116.

14. *Ibid.*, p. 71.

15. John A. T. Robinson, *Honest to God* (The Westminster Press, 1963), Ch. 4, pp. 64–83.

16. E. L. Mascall, *The Secularization of Christianity* (Holt, Rinehart and Winston, Inc., 1966). Mascall criticizes Robinson in Ch. 3, devoting 86 full-size pages to his negative assessment of Robinson's 141 paperback pages.

17. Paul van Buren, *The Secular Meaning of the Gospel* (The Macmillan Company, 1963).

18. Mascall, *op. cit.*, p. 155.

19. Karl Barth, *The Humanity of God* (John Knox Press, 1960).

20. Bonhoeffer, *Prisoner for God*, p. 179.

21. Bonhoeffer, *The Cost of Discipleship*, pp. 342, 344.

V. *The Rise of the Radicals*

1. Mircea Eliade, *Cosmos and History: The Myth of the Eternal Return* (Harper Torchbooks, 1959), p. 159, n. 15.

2. Gabriel Vahanian, *The Death of God* (George Braziller, Inc., 1961).

3. Thomas J. J. Altizer, *Oriental Mysticism and Biblical Eschatology* (The Westminster Press, 1961); *Mircea Eliade and the Dialectic of the Sacred* (The Westminster Press, 1963); *The Gospel of Christian Atheism* (The Westminster Press, 1966); and, with William Hamilton, *Radical Theology and the Death of God.*

4. Altizer, *Mircea Eliade and the Dialectic,* p. 13.

5. William Hamilton, *The New Essence.*

6. *Ibid.*, p. 30.

7. Van Buren, *op. cit.*

8. *Ibid.*, pp. 79, 100, 103.

9. See William Hamilton, *The New Essence,* pp. 35, 44, 49, 55

et passim; also, Altizer, *Oriental Mysticism,* pp. 162, 196; *Mircea Eliade and the Dialectic,* pp. 61, 107, 126 ff., 130, 172, 192.

10. Bonhoeffer, *No Rusty Swords,* pp. 27, 361–372.

11. Ludwig Feuerbach, *The Essence of Christianity,* pp. x–xxxii. Karl Barth has written an introductory essay to Feuerbach, saying that no philosopher of his time spoke with such pertinence about contemporary theological problems as he.

12. William Hamilton, *The New Essence,* pp. 36 ff.

13. *Ibid.,* p. 44.

14. Albert Camus, *The Plague,* tr. by Stuart Gilbert (Alfred A. Knopf, Inc., 1957).

15. William Hamilton, *The New Essence,* and the five essays by him, reprinted in Altizer and Hamilton, *Radical Theology and the Death of God.*

16. William Hamilton, *The New Essence,* p. 54.

17. Altizer and Hamilton, *op. cit.,* pp. 87 ff.

18. *Ibid.,* p. 90.

19. *Ibid.,* p. 92.

20. William Hamilton, *The New Essence,* p. 60.

21. *Ibid.,* pp. 60–61, and Augustine, *On True Religion,* XXIX, p. 73.

22. Tillich, *The Shaking of the Foundations,* p. 139. See also, William Hamilton, *The New Essence,* p. 62.

23. Karl Barth, *The Word of God and the Word of Man,* tr. by Douglas Horton (Harper Torchbooks, 1957). See esp. pp. 178–182.

24. *Ibid.,* p. 179.

25. William Hamilton, *The New Essence,* p. 63.

26. Altizer and Hamilton, *op. cit.,* p. xi. This soft interpretation is number seven in the ten possible meanings that Altizer and Hamilton suggest are possible interpretations of the phrase, " God is dead."

27. *Ibid.,* p. x. This radically unique interpretation is number two in Altizer's and Hamilton's description.

28. *The New Schaff-Herzog Encyclopedia of Religious Knowledge,* Vol. II, ed. by S. M. Jackson (Funk & Wagnalls Company, 1909), pp. 50–51.

29. Altizer, *The Gospel of Christian Atheism,* p. 11.

30. *Ibid.,* pp. 10–11.

31. Altizer and Hamilton, *op. cit.*, p. xii.

32. Harvey Cox is professor of theology at Harvard Divinity School and the author of *The Secular City*. Cox writes that the theology of Barth is better suited to the needs of man in the secular city than is that of Tillich (pp. 78–84).

33. Kenneth Hamilton, *op. cit.* Hamilton is professor of theology at the United College, Winnipeg, Canada. He is an extremely conservative Reformed theologian.

34. *Ibid.*, p. 236, n. 1.

35. Paul Tillich, *On the Boundary*.

36. Martin Kähler, *op. cit.* Tillich wrote an appreciative foreword to this translation of his teacher's work.

37. Paul Tillich, *Systematic Theology*, Vol. I, pp. 211 ff. See also Tillich, *The Courage to Be*, pp. 178–190.

38. Thomas A. O'Meara and C. D. Weisser (eds.), *Paul Tillich in Catholic Thought* (The Priory Press, 1964); George H. Tavard, *Paul Tillich and the Christian Message* (Charles Scribner's Sons, 1962); and George F. McLean, *Man's Knowledge of God According to Paul Tillich* (The Catholic University of America Press, 1958).

39. Tillich, *Systematic Theology*, Vol. II, pp. 148–150.

40. *Ibid.*, p. 123.

41. *Time*, Oct. 22, 1965, p. 62.

42. *U. S. News & World Report*, Apr. 18, 1966, p. 56.

43. Cox, *op. cit.*, p. 266. See also pp. 257–269.

44. Langdon P. Gilkey. Mimeographed paper read to the faculty conference of the Divinity School of the University of Chicago, 1964, partially published in *The Voice*, Crozer Theological Seminary, LVII, 1965, pp. 4–11.

45. *Ibid.*, p. 2 of the mimeographed paper.

VI.   *The Future of Theology*

1. William Hamilton, " The Death of God," *Playboy*, Vol. 13, No. 8 (Aug. 1966), p. 138.

2. *Ibid.*, p. 139.

3. *The Encyclopædia Britannica*, Vol. 16 (Chicago, 1966), pp. 695–696.

4. The boy (Eugene) in *Long Day's Journey Into Night*, an

autobiographical play not presented until two years after O'Neill's death, says this about himself. See the review of this play in *The Christian Century*, Vol. LXXIV (Feb. 20, 1957), p. 235.

5. See John C. Cooper, " Tragedy Without God," unpublished B. D. Thesis, The Lutheran Theological Southern Seminary, Columbia, S. C. (1957), p. 11. See also, *Representative Modern Plays: American*, ed. by Robert Warnock (Scott, Foresman & Company, 1952), p. 280.

6. Jean-Paul Sartre, *Situations, I*, Paris, 1947, p. 153, reported by W. Desan in *The Tragic Finale* (Harvard University Press, 1954), p. 179.

7. Warnock, *op. cit.*, pp. 280–281.

8. Barrett H. Clark, *Eugene O'Neill* (Robert M. McBride & Co., 1929), p. 192.

9. Eugene O'Neill, " The Lay of the Singer's Fall " (1912), reported in E. A. Engel, *The Haunted Heroes of Eugene O'Neill* (Harvard University Press, 1953), p. 299.

10. *The Collected Plays of Arthur Miller* (The Viking Press, Inc., 1957), p. 320.

11. Vahanian, *op. cit.*

12. *Ibid.*, p. xvii.

13. William Hamilton, " The Death of God," *Playboy*, p. 138.

14. Albert Camus, *Resistance, Rebellion, and Death* (Modern Library, 1960), p. 55.

15. Pierre Teilhard de Chardin, *The Phenomenon of Man* (Harper Torchbooks, 1961).

16. Pierre Teilhard de Chardin, *The Divine Milieu* (Harper Torchbooks, 1965).

17. Pierre Teilhard de Chardin, *The Future of Man* (Harper & Row, Publishers, Inc., 1964).

18. Nicolas Corte, *Pierre Teilhard de Chardin: His Life and Spirit* (The Macmillan Company, 1961), p. 56.

19. Teilhard de Chardin, *The Divine Milieu*, pp. 150–155.

20. *Ibid.*, p. 152.

21. *Ibid.*, p. 153.

22. Teilhard de Chardin, *The Future of Man*, pp. 214–237.

23. *Ibid.*, p. 279.

Date Due